A Pitcher of Cream

By

Bud Robinson

Author of
Sunshine and Smiles

ISBN 0-88019-354-9

Schmul Publishing Co., Inc.
Wesleyan Book Club   1996   Salem, Ohio

Printed by
Old Paths Tract Society
Route 2, Box 43
Shoals, IN 47581

Introduction

A Pitcher of Cream needs no introduction to the human family. All that is needed is a spoon and a corn pone, and we will do the rest.

BUDDIE.

BUD ROBINSON

Dedication

I lovingly dedicate this book to old Jessie, the best friend we ever had, who has provided us with Jersey milk and sweet cream for lo, these many years. If there is a land of perpetual clover where Jersey cows go, may old Jessie have an abundant entrance in.

Gratefully,

BUD ROBINSON.

Contents

A PITCHER OF CREAM

Skimmings

My friend, if the devil can succeed in skimming the cream off of your religious experience, he will leave you with a bowl of clabber on your hands; and, as you rattle your bowl and eat clabber with a brass spoon, you will imagine, because nobody wants your clabber, that you are the only fellow in all this land of ours that has the real thing.

Well, old boy, I don't propose to eat clabber and drink skimmed milk when I can get cream at the same price. My, my! neighbor, why should I put clabber or skimmed milk on my strawberries when the waiter is standing by with a smile on his face and a pitcher of cream in his hand, saying, "Help yourself, there is plenty more."

* * * *

The next women's club that is organized should have a bread tray for its insignia, a sifter for its handshake and a rolling-pin for its password, then it would not be long until a great many homes would be reformed.

* * * *

My friend, if you meet satisfaction coming down the road with a smile on his face, for the Lord's sake give him the right hand of fellowship.

* * * *

When joy comes in at the door laughing, trouble goes up the chimney growling, looking back over his shoulder, gritting his teeth and praying for the Lord to burn the house down over the head of his enemy, but, bless the Lord, such prayers are never answered.

*　*　*　*

Comfort is now on the throne devising plans by which he may retain his position. Well, amen. Who blames him for it? Not I.

*　*　*　*

My friend, if you have no light to put in your pitcher, fill it up with cream or honey, for the sake of the cause you represent. Don't carry a pitcher of bluejohn around with you. When Gideon broke his pitcher, what if he had found to his surprise that his pitcher had been full of vinegar mingled with gall instead of a light flashing. Do you think the enemy would have fled before him while he and his three hundred men shouted the sword of the Lord and of Gideon? Not by any means. You feed the hungry with cream, or drive the enemy with the light.

*　*　*　*

A presiding elder or station preacher burning tobacco and blowing blue smoke out of one side of their heads, while they crack jokes, would never make a man think of Moses and Aaron burning sweet incense to the God of Israel while all the host stood outside of the holy place and shouted for joy.

*　*　*　*

When a Methodist preacher smokes cigars, why does he draw the smoke down into his lungs? Why, he is trying to warm up his cold heart.

*　*　*　*

When a Methodist preacher smokes cigars, why does he blow the smoke out through his nose? Why, he is feeding the germs of depravity.

— 10 —

Words with stingers in them are the seeds of depravity, and will grow and flourish in soil that has never been cultivated, and will yield an abundant harvest at any season of the year.

* * * *

A wholly sanctified man is like a stalk of ribbon cane. He never heads out and he is full of juice from top to bottom and you can grind him at any season of the year and get sugar water.

* * * *

Why is it that the back seats of a church are so much softer than the front seats? Why, because they have so many more feathers on them, of course. Haven't you noticed that the back seats of a church are always covered with feathers?

* * * *

A man with his mouth full of Star Navy tobacco does not look like a golden pot full of heavenly manna, white like coriander seed, and the taste of it like wafers made with honey.

* * * *

A man can lift a bigger load on his knees than he can on his feet, and carry it further and hold out longer.

* * * *

When a man gets his eyes off of Jesus Christ and puts them on his feelings, if his feelings don't feel as he feels they ought to feel then he is liable to go to feeling of his feelings and backslide.

* * * *

When a man has an axe to grind he comes in at the front gate with a smile on his face and gives you a hearty handshake and says, "Luck to you, old boy," but after his axe is ground, he would not spit on you if you were to catch on fire.

The first step toward scriptural apostasy is to sacrifice divine order for carnal propriety and think the reason we don't shout any now is because we are better cultured than we used to be. My friend, a man in any age of the world or in any avocation of life with the Holy Ghost in him is at least liable to praise God with a loud voice anywhere on earth, or at any time of the day or night. No man can put the blessed Holy Ghost in the cradle of carnal security and rock him to sleep. The Holy Ghost never takes a nap, and the very fact that the church goes to sleep proves that the blessed Spirit is gone. He probably has been grieved away. He may never return to them again, although they may go on with their regular routine of church work year in and year out, and, because they are adding a few names to their church roll, they may think that God is well pleased with them, when it may be a sad fact that the Holy Ghost has not been there for years, and they may go on in their dead formality, strangers to God, and the covenant of Divine grace, without hope, and because of their refinement and culture and orderly conduct, may imagine themselves to be Bible Christians. Their only hope of heaven is based on the fact that they know how to do church work and that they can do everything with decency and in perfect order. My Lord, who will wake them up before the judgment day!

*　　*　　*　　*

My intellect conceived it; my eye saw it; my ear heard it; my heart cried for it, and my conscience leaped upon the throne of my soul and said, "You ought to have it," and my will grasped it by the hand and said, "It shall be done," and in the twinkling of an eye the blessed Holy Ghost whispered to my conscience and said, "Be thou clean," and immediately I was flooded with the sunbeams of glory and went to praising God for a full and complete salvation from all sin.

*　　*　　*　　*

Well, glory to Jesus, He satisfies me. Hallelujah! I am still ahead, and the creek is rising every minute and will soon be out of its banks, for Jordan overfloweth all its banks at harvest times, and the trash and dead wood are washed away and the soul seems so clean and fresh and heaven-like, that there seems to be nothing to do only to praise and glorify God for the fountain that was opened up in the house of King David for sin and for uncleanness. Well, I will just stop long enough to shout and get another breath and sing, "This wonderful stream of salvation, It never runs dry," for to be heaven-born, heaven-bound and heaven-filled is the finest thing the human mind can conceive of; for getting religion beats gold mines, oil wells, honey ponds, fritter trees or diamond fields.

*   *   *   *

When I see a Methodist preacher with a big chaw of tobacco between his upper and lower jaw, chawing and spitting, I always look at his feet to see if he has a forked hoof, for Moses said that any animal that chews his cud and did not have a forked hoof was an unclean beast and not fit for service.

*   *   *   *

A preacher that chews tobacco and smokes cigars may preach a gospel that will reach some souls and bring them to God, but while he is winning a few souls with his gospel, he is at least liable to damn as many or more with his influence than he saves with his gospel, and he himself may be saved yet so as by fire and his works will be burned up. See 1 Cor. 3:15.

A Pitcher of Cream

My friend, I am not able to give you a herd of cows, but bless the Lord, I am able to give you a Pitcher of Cream. Cream is to milk just what perfect love is to religion. It is that ingredient that makes it rich and juicy, and full of sweetness and nutrition.

Oh, my! just think of your boyhood days when Mother used to come up from that old spring house and skim the milk and leave a yellow streak around the top of the milk-pan.

My! My! What satisfaction a hungry boy found in licking the cream off the milk pan! He would live longer in ten minutes than he had all day. It just makes me hungry now to think of going by a spring house and, of course, I don't mean to drink up the milk, but just think of a hungry boy lifting the top off the milk pan and just sticking his finger down into the cream and licking his fingers as he goes up the hill.

Now, dear reader, if you have never tried to contrast the difference between different kinds of milk, you don't know what a job you would have on hands to try to do it. Now just think of the difference between cream and skimmed milk. Why, they are as far apart, as you and your dear old mother-in-law. You can see there is no fellowship between the two at all, and when you think of cream and buttermilk, it almost makes you feel like contrasting you and your bad neighbor, which you see is just out of all reason. No comparison in this world between you and your neighbors, and when you think of cream and clabber the English language just simply breaks down, and there is no word that you can use that will express the difference. From the time I started out in life, up to a few years ago, I would occasionally hear of some fellow calling me one of those clabber heads, and I have often wondered why nobody had ever called me cream head, but alas! my brother, alas! You see it is like this. When a man is known to be a clabber head and goes to any place, they expect him to "go away back and sit down," so you can see at once that the world is disgusted with clabber. Just why, I am not prepared to say now, I may tell you later on.

Now, when a fellow has been out on a preaching tour for from three to five months and takes his meals up town at one of those cafes, and when he lies down at night to sleep, his mind goes to wandering and finally he gets back to Mother and boyhood days, and he can just see himself coming in at night and sitting down on the old long bench, and Mother pushing toward him a bowl of cream, and a great big piece of old-fashioned cornbread, and a spoon, and the next thing in order is to crumble his bread into a bowl of cream, and in a few minutes the cream and bread begin to disappear. You might talk to that boy about a gold mine, and he would smile and tell you he had just struck one and it was very rich. You might tell him about a millionaire, and as he licked the cream off his lips, he would tell you that he was one of those things himself. I tell you, reader, when a fellow sits down to a bowl of cream and cornbread like Mother makes it, it is so good that it makes him want to live to be a hundred years old.

Now, reader, you will remember that all the good things you ever heard of were compared to cream. If a man preaches a great sermon, we say it was the very cream of the gospel. If we hear a great oration, we say it was the very cream of the English language, and we smile and say, "My, My," how he can throw the English together, but did you ever hear a good thing compared to clabber? No, and you never will.

The fact is, the blessing of perfect love will cause you to graze in the clover fields with the honey bees and climb the honeysuckle and sip honey with the hummingbirds, and just simply sit on the limbs of the trees and sing with the mockingbirds. Perfect love takes the stinger out of your tongue and the enmity out of your heart. It may not fill your purse and straighten out your head, but it will straighten your life and fill your heart and take all the fret and worry out of your life.

Another thing I find in my cup of cream is conviction, as deep as the demand of fallen humanity, and repentance clear out to the suburbs of my being; a faith that reaches clear up to heaven and takes hold on God, and demands a hearing in the city of light, and a justification for all my past guilt that sends me down the stream of time a happy man with a brand new pardon hung up in the gallery of my soul, and a regeneration that makes a living man out of a dead man, and restores me to the image and fellowship of God, and the blessed witness of the Holy Spirit with my spirit, that my sins are pardoned, that I am born of God; indeed, I am a new creature; old things are passed away, and, behold, all things are become new; I am adopted into the family of God as His son; an heir of heaven, a joint heir with the Lord Jesus Christ, and that my name is written in the Lamb's Book of Life.

I also find in this cream pitcher that God has provided for me the blessing of sanctification, which removes the last and least remains of sin out of my heart and cleanses away the depravity that caused me to commit the first sin I ever committed, that brought spiritual death to my soul, which is the groundwork for the new birth.

Well, praise God! What wonderful things we find when we get into a bowl of cream. The next thing I see floating on cream is glorification. Now, this blessed experience is the crowning blessing that comes to the child of God. This great blessing removes all the infirmities of the human body and prepares us for a home in the skies. Salvation has but one end to it, and that is the beginning. There is no need of but one spiritual birth in a lifetime, and indeed there should not be but one; converted once, sanctified once, and to settle the inbred sin question forever, so that from the time of the new birth we ought to grow and expand and rejoice all the rest of our lives, and praise God for an endless salvation. If we live up to the light that falls across our pathway, we will have new revelations from God every day of our lives.

The way of salvation is the only easy way in this world. When I was in the other way, I had to eat clabber and pull my hair and grit my teeth and think of committing suicide. No cream there, Honey. The devil makes a great hurricane, but his crowd is scattering the sand hills and drinking skimmed milk as sure as the man is in the moon.

Now the thing that satisfies the longing of the soul is this New Jerusalem cream, all flavored up with heavenly sunlight, and through this heavenly sunlight we are able to read our titles clear to mansions in the sky. Ah, reader, just think of walking on earth and reading your name in heaven, and you will see that you have stepped from nothing to everything, and from the bottom to the top, and from a bond slave of the devil to a son of God, from a pauper to a millionaire, and from a wretched, miserable, guilty, condemned, lost sinner to a loving, gentle child of God. And now, I do bless God for this one thought that comes rolling up in my mind and it is this: the reason that God paid such an enormous price for me was because He bought me to keep. He never bought me with any expectation of trading me off either in time or eternity, and if I am worth Fifteen Hundred Dollars for one year what would I be worth for all eternity! As you see, dear reader, that when our mind goes out to look for the other end of salvation we begin to reel and stagger like a drunken man, and we throw up our hands in amazement, and say of a truth salvation has but one end to it. Salvation and damnation are the only two things in existence that will never end. When we see a man filled with grace, and peace, and love, and mercy, we praise God as he runs up the shining way, leaping and blessing God, but when we see a man with his breath in his nose, and the judgment day is set, and all eternity hung up over his head, and see the awful monster death on his track like a bloodhound from the pit of woe, we throw up our hands in holy horror, and say, "My God, why don't he stop!" And God whispers to us and says, "He is blinded by the god of this world," and "led by the devil captive at his will," and he can't stop. He is a bondslave and driven under the lash of the devil. And the Lord says, how strange it seems when we see the sinner working so hard to build up and honor and glorify the devil, knowing them to be deadly enemies of each other. Then we are made to ask, why will a man give his time, money, talent to build up the cause of his enemy when he knows the devil will wreck him on earth, and finally damn him eternally in an awful hell?

Now, if men were in love with the devil, the problem would be solved, but where is the man who loves the devil; probably he can't be found on earth, or in heaven, or in hell, and that proves to me that the sinner is in an awful delusion. Will he ever wake up? I fear not.

I turned over my cream pitcher this morning and to my delight, it was full of precious stones. As they rolled over the floor, I picked them up and saw the face of Jesus Christ gleaming from every one of them, and also a verse of Scripture seemed to be engraved on each stone. The first one I picked up was so beautiful, it fairly dazzled my eyes, and as I looked through the sparkling stone, I saw the words "To wit, that God was in Christ, reconciling the world unto himself, not imputing their trespasses unto them; and hath committed unto us the word of reconciliation" II Cor. 5:19. O how my heart leaped for joy, as I read the words, "Not imputing their trespasses unto them." I said, glory to God! There is hope for the guilty, and pardon for the condemned. Hallelujah!

"All the fulness of the Godhead bodily" Col. 2:9. "For it pleased the Father that in him should all fulness dwell" Col. 1:19. "In whom are hid all the treasures of wisdom and knowledge" Col. 2:3. "And of his fulness have we all received, and grace for grace" John 1:16. "But when the fulness of the time was come, God sent forth his Son, made of a woman, made under the law, to redeem them that were under the law, that we might receive the adoption of sons. And because we are sons, God hath sent forth the Spirit of his Son into your hearts, crying, Abba, Father" Gal. 5:4, 5, 6. "Verily, verily, I say unto you, He that believeth on me hath everlasting life. I am that bread of life; your fathers did eat manna in the wilderness, and are dead. This is the bread which cometh down from heaven."

The next stone I picked up had these words on it, "For he whom God hath sent speaketh the words of God: for God giveth not the Spirit by measure unto him" John 3:34. The fact that God gave not the Spirit by measure to Christ, proves His greatness. It seems from this text that God has to measure the spirit to us and give it to us just like giving medicine, or just what He thinks we can stand.

Oh, how great is the Christ, God the Father in Him, and the Spirit not given by measure to Him. And He said He was in the world, and the world was made by Him. And without Him was not anything made that was made.

When I read the Scriptures on these two beautiful stones, my heart leaped for joy, and I picked up both hands full and commenced to read and read as follows: "Verily, verily, I say unto you, He that believeth on me hath everlasting life. I am that bread of life. Your fathers did eat manna in the wilderness, and are dead. This is the bread which cometh down from heaven, that a man may eat thereof, and not die. I am the living bread which came down from heaven: if any man eat of this bread, he shall live forever: and the bread that I will give is my flesh, which I will give for the life of the world" John 6:47-51. "Labour not for the meat which perisheth, but for that meat which endureth unto everlasting life, which the Son of man shall give unto you: for him hath God the Father sealed" John 6:27.

"In the last day, that great day of the feast, Jesus stood and cried, saying, If any man thirst, let him come unto me, and drink. He that believeth on me, as the scripture hath said, out of his belly shall flow rivers of living water. But this spake he of the Spirit, which they that believe on him should receive: for the Holy Ghost was not yet given; because that Jesus was not yet glorified" John 7:37-39. "And Jesus came and spake unto them, saying, All power is given unto me in heaven and in earth. Go ye, therefore, and teach all nations, baptizing them in the name of the Father, and of the Son, and of the Holy Ghost: teaching them to observe all things whatsoever I have commanded you:

and, lo, I am with you always, even unto the end of the world. Amen" Matt. 28:18-20. "Who being the brightness of his glory, and the express image of his person, and upholding all things by the word of his power, when he had by himself purged our sins, sat down on the right hand of the Majesty on high" Heb. 1:3.

"Who, being in the form of God, thought it not robbery to be equal with God: but made himself of no reputation, and took upon him the form of a servant, and was made in the likeness of men" Phil. 2:6, 7. "For unto us a child is born, unto us a son is given; and the government shall be upon his shoulder: and his name shall be called Wonderful, Counsellor, The Mighty God, The Everlasting Father, The Prince of Peace. Of the increase of his government and peace there shall be no end, upon the throne of David, and upon his kingdom, to order it, and to establish it with judgment and with justice from henceforth even for ever. The zeal of the Lord of hosts will perform this" Isa. 9:6, 7. "The Spirit of the Lord God is upon me; because the Lord hath anointed me to preach good tidings unto the meek; he hath sent me to bind up the broken hearted, to proclaim liberty to the captives, and the opening of the prison to them that are bound; to proclaim the acceptable year of the Lord, and the day of vengeance of our God; to comfort all that mourn; to appoint unto them that mourn in Zion, to give unto them beauty for ashes, the oil of joy for mourning, the garment of praise for the spirit of heaviness; that they might be called trees of the righteousness, the planting of the Lord, that he might be glorified" Isa. 61:1, 2, 3. "I gave my back to the smiters, and my cheeks to them that plucked off the hair: I hid not my face from shame and spitting" Isa. 50:6. "He shall see of the travail of his soul, and shall be satisfied: by his knowledge shall my righteous servant justify many; for he shall bear their iniquities" Isa. 53:11. "Who is this that cometh from Edom, with dyed garments from Bozrah? this that is glorious in his apparel, travelling in the greatness of his strength? I that speak in righteousness, mighty to save" Isa. 63:1.

Ladies and gentlemen, no doubt, the most of you have heard that I was from Texas, and oh! how it thrills my heart with joy to think that I am from the "Lone Star" State, the greatest of all states, Texas. It is a fact not generally understood that Texas has been Texas ever since the creation of the earth, although the name was not attached to it until recent years.

Texas has more land and fewer people, more cows and less milk, more creeks and less water, more bees and less honey, more wind and less money than any other state. Texas is, however, a broad plot of land, lying in between Boston, Mass. and Old Mexico. Texas has had a hard name saddled on it; nevertheless, Texas was not to blame for its hard name that was brought about by its surroundings. You see, Texas was surrounded on the west by the Mexicans, on the north by the Indians, and on the east by the Arkansans, and of course, you are all ready to admit that the most of us are controlled to a great extent by our surroundings, and the surroundings of Texas were enough to give this great state the blue jaundice, much less a hard name; nevertheless the foundation of Texas standeth sure. We have some peculiar things in Texas I grant you, to see trees with thorns on them, and the cattle with horns on them, and the people all mulies is somewhat a mystery. Nevertheless the Texans are natural born mulies. The interesting fact about the Texan is that they are called the long-horns and at the same time they are mulies. Now a Texan is as great a curiosity as a Chinaman, and the Chinaman is said to be the greatest curiosity on earth, from the fact that his head and tail are both on the same end, and the natural born Texan is a long-horned mulie.

* * * *

We have a full salvation on a rock foundation and we are going to shout it all over this nation. See what a difference between two words, *eternal life* and *eternal death*, and the first seven letters in each word the same. There is nothing that the human mind can conceive of that is good but what is found in the words eternal life, and there is nothing that is awful and horrible but what is found in eternal death. One means delivered from all sin; the other means damned eternally; and *delivered* and *damned* both begin with the letter "d."

* * * *

Some men can stand on the street corner and chew and smoke by the hour and crack jokes and jaw back at every passerby; that night if he gets out to prayer meeting and you call on him to pray he will beg to be excused, and tell you that he is suffering much with one of his lungs.

* * * *

Well, now brother, if you had not told us of your weak lung we probably never would have found it out, for you talked so loud on the streets today that really we are surprised to know that one of your lungs is affected. Now, when you go back downtown tomorrow, you had better watch that lung of yours, for that old affected lung is liable to get you into an awful lot of trouble at the judgment day.

* * * *

The difference between folks is just the difference between you and me. Do you catch on to that? But you say, "But Bro. Robinson, the folks—"? Yes, and I say, "You, you, you, you," and then you turn and look at me and say, "You," and I turn and look at you and say, "You."

* * * *

Some men would rather wallow in sin for forty years and die like a beast and be blotted out of existence forever than to be a refined, cultured Christian gentleman for forty years and die in faith and go to heaven and live with the pure forever. If that don't look like total depravity, I wonder what kind of glasses you are looking through.

* * * *

My friend, if you don't get religion, the devil will get you, and if you don't turn sin loose, God will turn you loose. Some men say they just chew tobacco for pastime. Well, my friend, I met time just after you had been chewing and you had spit ambeer all over him, and old time sure did look awful filthy. It looks to me like if you had had any respect for your passing guest you would not have spit on him.

* * * *

My friend, if you are not willing to be taught, you can never teach; and if you are not willing to obey, you can never command; and if you are not willing to follow, you can never make a leader.

* * * *

The most soul-stirring, heart-melting, uplifting satisfaction that ever comes to the heart and life of the child of God is to sit down in the church on Sunday morning and listen to the pastor preach on the subject of religion; but one of the most disgusting, heart-rending, soul-sickening, disappointing things on earth is to go to your church on Sunday morning with a hungry soul and expect to be fed from the King's table and hear the learned doctor discourse on the subject of "Our Nation's Owning and Controlling the Telegraph and Telephone Poles."

* * * *

Well, now, children, if you have got a satisfactory, satisfied satisfaction hung up all over your soul, it means that God has made you perfect in love, but if you have received hundreds of big blessings, *but*; and the Lord has given you as good an experience as anybody, *but*; and you have been blessed nearly to death a number of times, *but*; and you would not ask the Lord for anymore, *but*; it just means that you have not got the experience of perfect love and there is no use in your spending any more money on your well curbing, but get your pick and shovel and go down into your well and dig it several feet deeper and you will strike the overflow, and it will flow out at the top and drown out all your *"buts."*

What strange "critters" we mortals be! Strange indeed, yes indeed. To hear a fellow shout loud one day, to hear him flaunt much the second day, to hear him growl on the third day, to hear him talk about this neighbors on the fourth day, to hear him grumble and whine about the weather on the fifth day, to see him pout with his wife and children on the sixth day, and hear him proffer everything in the New Testament on the seventh day, we wonder what turn he would take if our weeks had eight days in them. Well, this fellow beats the vision that Ezekiel saw.

Ezekiel saw a fellow with four faces, but here is a fellow with seven; a new face for every day in the week. Oh! man, great is thy gullibility! Thou art a seven-faced monster.

My Birthright

Conviction that reaches clear down to the bottom of my soul, repentance that reaches clear out to the suburbs of my being, a faith that reaches clear up to heaven, justification for all my guilt and condemnation, sanctification for all my impurities, glorification for all my infirmities and a heaven filled with the pure and good where Jesus Christ reigns supreme to enjoy forever. Oh! Glory! Isn't it grand? Saved from all sin for all time to come and saved to all grace through all eternity. Well, glory to Jesus, didn't I make a trade that will put a shine on me when the world is on fire, and the ungodly will cry for the rocks and mountains to fall on them and hide them from the face of Him that sitteth on the throne, when they could have had as much and maybe more than I have, just for the taking of it. See what they have missed! I tell you, children, if the dear Lord don't want me to graze in His pasture, He had better not go off and leave His gate open, for if He does, when He comes back, He will find me in clover and bluegrass up to my eyes and looking through the clover blossoms, smiling at Him as He comes in, and He will find me sleek, fat and with honey dew all over my soul, and eating clover and reading my title clear to mansions in the sky. One of the happiest of the happy and fullest of the full.

Do you understand? This is glorious!

New England in a Nutshell

I am often asked what I think of New England. Well, I think New England is a wonderful combination. They feed their physical man on beefsteak, baked beans, baker's bread and malted milk. They feed their mental man on Greek roots, Latin verbs and Hebrew phrases. They only feed their spiritual man once a week and that is generally on Sunday morning. Their Sunday meal consists of a half teacup of higher criticism, seasoned with a tablespoon full of Unitarianism, flavored with a teaspoon full of Universalism, with Christian Science sprinkled on to suit the taste; they have fifteen minutes to take their prescription in, and they serve it cold.

*   *   *   *

Well, after talking with some of my friends, I just want to ask a question. Is a man a rascal who borrows trouble without any expectation of ever paying back? Is that getting goods under false pretenses? If so, some people ought to be dealt with according to the thirteenth chapter of Ist Corinthians.

*   *   *   *

If the devil can succeed in getting me to grieve over yesterday and be uneasy about tomorrow, he has robbed me of my today, and left me stranded on the banks of time like the driftwood of a swollen stream.

*   *   *   *

Two of the brightest stars in my crown are peace and contentment. They yield perfect satisfaction and the fullness of joy, and these graces all grow on the tree of life when it is planted in the redeemed soul.

Some Beautiful Things From the Old Testament

We read in Psalm 68:13, "Though we have lien among the pots, yet shall ye be as the wings of a dove covered with silver, and her feathers with yellow gold." We next notice in Job 22:23-28, "If thou return to the Almighty, thou shalt be built up, thou shalt put away iniquity far from thy tabernacles. Then shalt thou lay up gold as dust, and the gold of Ophir as the stones of the brooks. Yea, the Almighty shall be thy defence, and thou shalt have plenty of silver. For then shalt thou have thy delight in the Almighty, and shalt lift up thy face unto God. Thou shalt make thy prayer unto him, and he shall hear thee, and thou shalt pay thy vows. Thou shalt also decree a thing and it shall be established unto thee: and thy light shall shine upon thy ways."

*   *   *   *

Three drunkards to deal with instead of one. I suppose it will be generally admitted that the nicotine drunkard is the commonest drunkard of all the drunkards in the land. As surely as opium has cursed China and left its blighting and withering hand on their children, and robbed them of their God and manhood without one ray of hope, and left their whole land and nation in darkest heathenism, so the tobacco curse has swept down on the enlightened people of Christian America, and has robbed millions of them of their manhood, and today in this enlightened land of ours, a cigarette sucker or a cigar smoker will walk right up face to face with a stranger and burn his rotten poison tobacco and blow the smoke into the face of a man, and, as far as I can see, have no more conception of doing wrong than anything in the world. Any thinking man can see that they are absolutely robbed of all the principles of manhood, and they are as dead to the spirit of common decency and the Spirit of Jesus Christ as any heathen in

China or Africa. At least seventy-five per cent of the young men in my state today are robbed of manhood and have no higher idea of life and its responsibility than an ordinary Chinaman. There is nothing that seems to satisfy them only a pouch of smoking tobacco and a roll of brown paper and a box of sulphur matches and a crowd of them to get together on the street corner and smoke and curse and tell filthy jokes. They are not fit to make husbands and fathers out of, and they are not prepared to make merchants, or doctors, or statesmen, or preachers.

Well, what on earth can we make out of them? We will have to make beasts of burden out of them. They will have to work in the slime pits and make brick without straw and be driven by the lash of the taskmaster. Why? Because they are slaves. They have sold themselves for naught, and today our beautiful land is loaded down to the water-line with opium drunkards, nicotine drunkards, alcohol drunkards, and the commonest drunkards of all drunkards is the tobacco drunkard. Of course, a tobacco-using church member will excuse himself and say, "I am not as bad as the other fellow." Well, let us see about that. The opium eater eats opium for the effect it has on him. The church member says, "Well, yes, of course, that is the reason he eats it." Well, now let us take another step. The alcohol drunkard drinks alcohol for the effect it has on him. "Well, yes," says the church member, "that is true." Well, now let us take the third step. A tobacco-using church member uses tobacco for the effect it has on him. Now, church member, how can you put one poor slave in hell for eating opium for the effect it had on him, and another poor slave in hell for drinking alcohol for the effect it had on him, and at the same time put the other slave in heaven for using tobacco for the effect it had on him. There is not an angel in heaven or a saint on earth that can tell the difference between these three drunkards, only they both know that the tobacco drunkard is the filthiest drunkard of the three. We have often noticed in our work that the new birth will cure the alcohol drunkard, but the new birth will not cure the nicotine drunkard, and if a man ever gets rid of nicotine tobacco, he is going to have more grace than people get in the new birth, for it is a stubborn fact that most all church members and I suppose that at least seventy-five per cent. of the preachers of the South use tobacco. Now, if the new birth cures the tobacco disease then we must suppose that most of the preachers and the great bulk of the church members have never been converted at all; but I suppose that most all church members have at some time been converted, although they have chewed and squirted tobacco juice on the floor and on the walls and out the windows of God's house until God has become disgusted with their filth, and has withdrawn Himself from them until they are today in a backslidden state. It is real sad to hear them talk about old-time religion. Well, so they remember the time when Jesus in His fullness and sweetness came into their hearts and took the burden away, but instead of their cleaning up and living a clean life, they went right on chewing and smoking and getting drunk on nicotine, and the Son of God will not stay in the heart of a drunkard, and to their sad surprise, they have waked up to the awful fact that the Christ of Calvary is not there at all, and all they seem to have now is a memory of what they used to have, and they talk of old-time religion, and don't seem to realize that Christ is as loving and gentle today as He was twenty years ago.

The difference is not in the blessed Christ, for we read that "He is the same yesterday, to day, and for ever," but God gives His children light to walk in and not to play with, and no child of God in this enlightened age can chew and smoke with a good conscience, and I have never spoken to a church member about the use of tobacco but that he tried to defend himself in the use of it, and would show color and get nervous and seem to get excited about it. Now, if they were willing to talk about it in a reasonable way, and confess that although they used it, they did not think it to be the right thing, they would at least keep quiet and feel easy while they talked on the subject. I have seen preachers turn white and look deathly pale while they tried to defend the use of tobacco, and would get so wrought up that they hardly knew what they were saying, and while they were pale and nervous and excited, would say they never had been convicted that it was wrong, when every word they said and every action proved to the thinking mind that they were at that moment under conviction that they were doing wrong. I am fully convinced in my mind that a saloon keeper has as much scriptural ground to defend the saloon, as a preacher has the cigar factory. It may be possible that the saloon is doing more to damn the boys of our country than the cigar stand, but I am almost persuaded in my mind that the hardest class of young men to reach is the perpetual smoker. Young men have smoked until they have drowned their consciences, and they can sit and listen to a gospel message and giggle all the time, and have no more sense of conviction than if they did not have a soul to be saved or eternally lost.

Oh, Man! with your breath in your nose and the judgment day set, and eternity hanging out before you, and old monster death on your track like a hound, will you not stop long enough to consider the awful danger in rejecting God's love and mercy? for God says, "Turn ye from your evil ways, for why will ye die the death that never dies? Awake! Awake! Ye sinners!

My Reasons for Believing in Scriptural Holiness

We read in I Peter 3:15, "But sanctify the Lord God in your hearts: and be ready always to give an answer to every man that asketh you a reason of the hope that is in you with meekness and fear." My first reason for believing in scriptural holiness is because it is an old doctrine. It is not a new fangled religion, as some would have you believe. It was not hatched out of the nest eggs of mere circumstances, nor did it spring up in the night like a mushroom. I have searched the scriptures with a craving mind and a longing soul and a hungry heart to find out about this doctrine of scriptural holiness. As far as I am able to see, there is nothing in existence as old as scriptural holiness, and for a proof text, we read in Paul's letter to the Ephesians the first chapter and fourth verse: "According as he hath chosen us in him before the foundation of the world, that we should be holy and without blame before him in love." The reader will notice that this text goes back before the foundation of the world. Now, my friend, I don't know how to go back to the beginning of holiness, but to my mind, at least, this is an old doctrine, and how people can talk of holiness as a new doctrine is a mystery to me inexplainable, for the text declares that it was God's choice before the foundation of the world that we should be holy and without blame before Him in love. Now, if this doctrine is true at all, it goes back beyond John Wesley, or George Fox, or Pentecost, or Abraham, or even the garden of Eden. Without a doubt, or a gainsaying voice this doctrine is true, for it had its beginning with God. Therefore, it is as old as God and as everlasting as eternity, and on this ground I say it is an old doctrine, and get to shouting victory through the blood of the blessed Son of God for the experience of scriptural holiness.

My next reason for believing in scriptural holiness is found in I. Thess. 4:3, "For this is the will of God, even your sanctification." Now, my friend, the very fact that God wills you the blessed experience of sanctification proves to my mind that you can get it. Why would an All-wise Heavenly Father will something to His children that they could not get, or that He did not have for them? It does not look reasonable to a thinking mind that God would do such a thing; and the very fact that He wills the blessing to us, forever settles the question about the children of God getting the blessing of scriptural holiness.

I now hasten on and give you my third reason for believing in scriptural holiness. We read in I Peter 1:15, 16, "But as he which hath called you is holy, so be ye holy in all manner of conversation; because it is written, Be ye holy; for I am holy." The reader will remember that in the first text it was God's choice, and in the second text it was His will, and now in this text it is God's command. He says "Be ye holy; for I am holy." You see the only reason God gives us is that He Himself is holy. He says nothing about our church or our creeds, or what our forefathers believed and taught, but when God told us to be holy, He thought we would obey Him, and He made no provisions for he fellow that stands back and says, "Well, my church has left holiness out of its creed." God's voice will come to him in thunder tones, "Be ye holy; for I am holy," and this command reaches all classes in all ages of the world, and this blessed old doctrine is being preached all over the world, for which I thank God, and take courage and press on preaching to a lost world a gospel full and free and for all classes on earth, feeling that God meant what He said when He said, "Be ye holy; for I am holy," and I feel I would not be worthy a place in His kingdom, if I were to go out and tell the people that they could not be made holy, and live a holy life.

We next notice my fourth reason for believing in scriptural holiness: We read in Acts 20:32, "And now, brethren, I commend you to God, and to the word of His grace, which is able to build you up, and to give you an inheritance among all them which are sanctified." Now, we have come to a beautiful thought in the lesson. The apostle says that the children of God inherit the blessing of sanctification; or to make it real plain, the experience of sanctification is the birthright of the child of God, and if so, every regenerated soul on earth is an heir to this wonderful experience of holiness, and should come immediately to his Heavenly Father and put in a claim for his part of this wonderful estate. Why in the world will people stay away when the Lord tells them in the Old Book that their inheritance is the blessing of sanctification, and that they are lawful heirs, and have a perfect right to their heirship, and that men or devils can't keep them out of it, if they are willing to come to Him and get in possession of their own estate.

Well, Amen. I have put in a claim, and the dear Lord delivered the goods to me. Bless His dear name! People don't know when they see me strut and grin what I am smiling about, but I know it is because I have gotten in possession of my estate, and now I am walking in Texas and living in heaven; for, you remember, Paul said our conversation is in heaven from whence we look for the Saviour, the Lord Jesus Christ, and the question is, how could a man's conversation be in heaven if he himself did not stay pretty close around there?

Well, we next notice my fifth reason: We read in Heb. 13:12, 13, "Wherefore Jesus also, that he might sanctify the people with his own blood, suffered without the gate. Let us go forth therefore unto him without the camp, bearing his reproach." Now, reader, if God, the Father, willed you the blessing, and God, the Son, died to accomplish it, it looks like men could get it. How could it be made plainer? I see no reason why men should not go in for all the fullness of God, when we have such statements as the above, "Jesus Christ suffered without the gate" to sanctify the people with His own blood. Now, reader, that beats growing into it, or waiting to die to get into it. You see the text says that Jesus Christ is to do the thing Himself. Now, the prophet Isaiah said concerning Jesus Christ that He shall never fail, nor be discouraged. Now, the Christ that shall never fail is the One that shed His blood to sanctify the people; and to reject the experience of sanctification is not by any means rejecting man, or a man-made theory of a something you know nothing about, but to reject it means to be a blood rejecter and a Christ despiser. But people say, "Oh, I don't reject Christ and His blood, I only reject sanctification," but the text says that "Jesus Christ suffered without the gate" to sanctify the people with His own blood; and, reader, there is no way around the fact, if the Son of God died to sanctify you and you reject sanctification, you are a blood-rejecter as sure as Christ died on the cross. It may be possible that you have for several years been rejecting the experience of sanctification because you did not believe some man's theory of the thing, but you lay down men's theories and come to the Old Book and see where you really are. If the Son of God died to sanctify you and you refuse to let Him do it, you are rejecting the death of the Son of God, and the devil is making you believe that you are only rejecting a man-made theory. Now, look down into your heart and see if Jesus Christ has ever really sanctified you, and the probabilities are that you will find a sad, hungry heart craving the experience of scriptural holiness, and at the same time rejecting it on the grounds that you object to your theory of the thing. Now, every man, I suppose, has some theory of sanctification, and, dear readers, if your theory has never yet gotten you into the experience, I am of the opinion that your theory is no good, and, at least, you had better try another one; if the road you travel never gets you to town, you are on the wrong road.

Now, my sixth reason for believing in scriptural holiness is found in Heb. 10:14, 15, 16, "For by one offering he hath perfected for ever them that are sanctified. Whereof the Holy Ghost also is a witness to us: for after that he had said before, This is the covenant that I will make with them after those days, saith the Lord, I will put my laws into their hearts, and in their minds will I write them." Now, friend, this text in connection with two of the others forever settle the question of whether we can be sanctified or not. One text said that God willed it to us, and the other one said that Christ died to sanctify us with His own blood, and this one said that the Holy Ghost witnesses to it. Now just look at these three texts for a minute and go down after the blessing. You see, if God willed it, and Christ died to accomplish it, and the blessed Holy Ghost witnesses to us that the thing is done, that forever settles it in three worlds; that it is done, and that it can be done. Well, glory to my Christ! Is it not grand? Now, reader, as surely as the Holy Ghost witnesses to the justified man that his sins are forgiven, the same blessed Holy Ghost witnesses to the child of God that he is sanctified wholly and cleansed from all unrighteousness. There is no use for any more battle ground if the Holy Ghost witnesses to us that the thing is done. We may just throw our spoons away and jump into the river and go to shouting, for we know if the thing was not done the Holy Ghost would not witness to it, for He would not witness to a thing that was not done.

My seventh reason for believing in scriptural holiness is found in Heb. 2:11. "For both he that sanctifieth and they who are sanctified are all of one: for which cause he is not ashamed to call them brethren." This text shows that a sanctified man stands well in heaven.

Now, dear reader, if you can get a religious experience that will cause you to stand well in heaven, and God will not be ashamed of you, surely you ought to have it. What in the world would be more desirable than to be in such harmony with the Lord that He would not be ashamed of us. Now, reader, if you seek and obtain the blessed experience of scriptural holiness, many of your friends and loved ones will be ashamed of you and will have nothing to do with you, and they will even make you feel like you have disgraced yourself and them by making such a profession, but if the God of heaven is not ashamed of you, you can well afford to stand the ridicule of a man with his breath in his nose if you stand well with the Judge of the whole earth. Holiness is about the only thing I know of that people are ashamed of, and yet it is the only thing a man has to have, or stay out of heaven.

The text says, "For both he that sanctifieth and they who are sanctified are all of one." Now, reader, the only people that the Bible says are at one with God are the people that God hath sanctified, and the same text says that He is not ashamed of them, and that proves that He is ashamed of the people who refuse to let Him sanctify them. No other conclusion can be reached, for if the Lord is not ashamed of a sanctified man, then He must be ashamed of the man who is not sanctified.

My eighth reason for believing in scriptural holiness is found in Heb. 12:14, "Follow peace with all men, and holiness, without which no man shall see the Lord." This text of Scripture forever shuts the mouth of the gainsayer, and puts a padlock on the jaw of the worldly church member, for without any preliminaries, or ifs, or ands about it, God just tells us that "without holiness no man shall see the Lord," and that forever settles the question.

Now, old boy, we have to go down and get holiness, or go up and hear the Lord say, "Depart from me, ye workers of iniquity, I know you not," and we can't afford to go to the judgment bar of God with a shadow of doubt over us; we must have clear sunlight in our souls so that when we reach the pearly portals, we will hear Him say, "Well done, thou good and faithful servant, ye have been faithful over a few things, I will make thee ruler over many things; enter thou into the joy of thy Lord."

Well, Amen. It is wonderful to know that God through Jesus Christ has opened up a way for our escape, and, bless His dear name, He has not only devised a plan by which we can escape sin, but He has opened up a way, by which we are to be made holy and enjoy it while we live, and carry it to heaven with us when we go to heaven.

Some people seem to think that we are to get holiness after we get to heaven, but, reader, we must have it before we get there, for God says, if we have not got it, we can't see Him, and that proves to any thinking mind that we have go to have holiness before we leave here, in order to see God when we get there. It may be possible that you have been talking about holiness cranks; that it was impossible to get it, impossible to live it, that nobody on earth ever did live it, and all such talk as that; but now, old boy, look up and see the text: "Without holiness no man shall see the Lord." You may say "bosh" and "sweet wind" to such talk, but you must remember that Jesus Christ said, "The heavens and the earth will pass away, but my word shall not pass away." Now, just turn to the Word and read there in letters of fire, "Follow peace with all men, and holiness, without which no man shall see the Lord."

My ninth reason for believing in scriptural holiness is found in the fact that when a man gets sanctified, it cleanses him from the use of tobacco. It is a well-known fact that when men get the blessed experience of holiness they unload their tobacco. I have never known one to fail. Of course, I have seen a few people that got the experience and refused to give up their tobacco, and every one of them lost their experience; that proves that the Holy Ghost will have a clean temple or He will not stay. I have known men and women to get sanctified, and would run on for a day or two, and think nothing of giving up the use of tobacco, and the Holy Ghost would make it so real to them that they must give up tobacco, there was no mistake in the world about it. They knew that it was the voice of the Holy Ghost, and if they use it any more it would be in direct opposition to the voice of the Lord; then if they went on and used it, they always backslid. I have preached over nearly forty states and can say of a truth of the holiness folks, to a man or woman are the cleanest set of folks I ever saw. But somebody will say, "Oh, I know a man that claims to be sanctified, and he uses tobacco." Well now, reader, the very fact that you say the fellow claims to have it, proves to my mind that you don't really think that he has got the blessing. You never see a truly sanctified man going down the streets of the city with a cigar in his mouth and you never will; he either cleans up, or goes back—one or the other.

My tenth reason for believing in scriptural holiness is found in the fact that it makes Prohibitionists out of us. Now, it is a fact that the holiness people North, South, East and West, rich or poor, vote the Prohibition ticket. The holiness people are without a doubt the cleanest and straightest crowd on earth—they are opposed to tobacco and liquor in any form. They are, as a people, free from tobacco, free from liquor and free from all kinds of secret lodges. I have known a great many men to get the experience of scriptural holiness and ninety-nine out of every one hundred never attend their lodges again. A holiness man with judgment don't go around clubs and lodges, but he withdraws from them, and walks with God the rest of his life. Of course, we don't claim that every man who votes the Prohibition ticket is a holiness man, but even to lay aside religion, the men who vote the Prohibition ticket are the cleanest set of men in the land; to say nothing of the great holiness movement, the men in the Prohibition party are the very cream of the church. You take a man in the church who chews and smokes tobacco and laughs at holiness, you never see him voting the Prohibitionist ticket; you will find him on every election day with a crowd of half-drunk Democrats, or Republicans and they smoke and chew and tell vulgar yarns and vote for some bloated-faced toper. You will find that to be the case in nine cases out of every ten. I have watched them for twenty-five years, and speak out of my experience, and not with a prejudiced mind at all.

Now, my friends, you can gather up my reasons for believing in scriptural holiness, and put them together and make you a charm string out of them. It was God's choice; it is God's will; it is God's command; it is your birthright; Jesus Christ died to accomplish it; the Holy Ghost witnesses to it; God is not ashamed of you if you have it; without it you can't see God; it cleans up the tobacco habit, makes a Prohibitionist out of the fellow who enjoys it.

Now, the ten reasons are all scriptural and reasonable. Now, can the reader give me ten reasons for not believing in scriptural holiness as good and as reasonable and as scriptural as these ten? If so, please write them out and mail them to Bud Robinson, Peniel, Tex.

Salvation

Salvation means deliverance; delivered from the devil, disgusted with the world, and sick of sin; my back is to the past and my face to the future, with joy in my soul and a heart full of perfect love, with a future as long as eternity and a hope as bright as heaven—this is salvation or deliverance from sin. I tell you, folks, when I traded for this thing I sure made a trade, and came out ahead, and who would have thought that of me? Why, nobody ever expected me to come to anything at all. Well, hallelujah! just look what came to me!

The folks that know things tell me that a fortune comes to every man's door once in a lifetime and knocks for admittance. Well, Glory to God! I was at home when he came, and I met him at the door and said, "Come in, Fortune, I am glad to see you, I have been looking for you ever since I was born. I wish to travel with you as long as I live in this world, and as long as I stay in the next one."

Well, "Glory to God in the highest, and on earth peace, good will toward men!" I have just found out that my fortune only had one end to it, and that was the beginning end, and as the ages roll by, my fortune will unfold and grow brighter and richer, and my soul will expand and drink in more and more of this salvation from sin, which is eternal life, which means just old-fashioned, good common-sense religion, the kind a fellow gets down in the straw, when he repents of all his sins, and confesses them out to God, and turns away from them, believing on the Lord Jesus Christ.

Now, this is surely salvation or deliverance from all sin. The man that is saved from all sin can reach God with one hand and a lost world with the other, and pull down grace and glory into the hearts of the people; for it is a fact the man that can reach heaven can reach his neighbor, and if a man can't reach heaven, he can't reach anybody, and his prayers fall like the autumn leaves and lie dead and lifeless on the cold ground. But how different it is to hear a man pray when you just feel every word burning its way through the sky, and at the same time burning its way through your heart.

If church membership should prove to be the standard at the judgment day, there would not be a vacant room in the new Jerusalem, but if holiness was to happen to be the standard the Lord would require at our hands, there would be whole blocks vacant throughout eternity, for almost all people of every tribe and tongue and nation have some form of religious worship and belong to the church, but people are so scarce that live holy that they are greatly in the minority. Nothing so popular as church membership, and nothing so unpopular as to be holy in the church. At one time, I thought the church belonged to the Lord, and that everybody in it had religion. I thought the devil had nothing to do with the church, but the time came when I had to change my opinion, for I found out to my surprise that the devil was in the church and almost run it to suit himself. I know some people will dispute this statement, but if you want to see whether the devil is in the church or not, you go into a church and say a few words about being holy and you will see the devil with real hoofs and horns, and that he is so entrenched in the church that it is impossible to root him out. Of course, I know of a few churches that believe in and preach and enjoy scriptural holiness, but the great bulk of our churches are not in sympathy with holiness, or the second coming of the Lord, or Divine healing, or anything that is spiritual. In a church of more than 1,000 members in one of the leading cities in America, I was told by about 500 of the members that if it took the new birth to make a man a Christian, they did not have any religion, and never had any. They told me face to face that if what I preached was religion, they were still in their sins. They were good, clever people and members of the church in good standing, and without a knowledge of saving grace. One man in a kind, brotherly way told me that he could do as good church work as anybody and that if he had ever been converted he had no knowledge of the fact.

The Sanctified Man

A man wholly sanctified is as bold as a lion. He neither fears men nor devils. He is as patient as an ox; he is patient with his friends, and he is patient with his enemies. He endures hardness as a good soldier of Jesus Christ. He is as swift as an eagle, he just touches the earth in the high places and he builds his nest on the Rock of Ages. He is as wise as a serpent; he shuns the very appearance of evil. He is as gentle as a lamb; he is easy to be entreated and you can warm up to him and he will warm up to you. He is as harmless as a dove; he is clean both inside and outside and he never strikes back either with his tongue or pen; he is as sweet as honey. If you were to stick your walking stick between his ribs, it would drip honey for a week.

A man wholly sanctified has a religious experience as deep as the demand of fallen humanity, as broad as the compassion of God, as high as heaven, and as everlasting as the Rock of Ages. He is delivered from all sin; he is filled with all the fullness of God; he has heaven in his eye and glory in his soul and a through ticket to the New Jerusalem, stamped with the blood of the Lamb, and in letters of fire written with the finger of God, "No stopovers allowed."

A man wholly sanctified has God for his Father, and Jesus Christ for his Saviour and Sanctifier, and the Holy Ghost for his Abiding Comforter, the angels for his companions, the redeemed saints of all ages for his brothers and sisters, and heaven for his eternal home. What a fortune!

A man wholly sanctified has a level head, a big soul, a good religious experience, a tender heart, a forgiving spirit, a loving disposition, a winning way, a power to draw, a clean record, an honest face. He is not lazy nor sluggish, nor slothful; he has got the get-up-and-get in his soul; he has the respect both of his friends

Glory!.

and his enemies; his enemies will respect him and hate him, while his friends will respect him and love him. He is a man of prayer and faith and he shows his faith by his works. He seems to have more time than anybody else; he has time for family prayers, time for prayer meetings, time for church, and then plenty of time to do all his work, and yet he seems to never be in a hurry.

*　　*　　*　　*

The blessed Son of God was the greatest bread breaker this world has ever heard of. He blessed five barley loaves and brake and fed not less than twelve or fifteen thousand people. The Bible says five thousand men, besides women and children; a paper sack full to start in with; many thousand people fed; twelve baskets full left over. He first blessed; second, He brake; third, He fed the multitude; fourth, the disciples went to gathering up and filling baskets with the fragments. I am persuaded that even Peter, James and John were amazed and said, "Did you ever see the like?" And of course, they never had, for nothing else had ever happened just like it. Moses gave the law and King David sang the hymns and Isaiah prophesied, but it took Christ to break bread.

*　　*　　*　　*

My friend, if you claim to love me at all, for the Lord's sake and for my sake and for your own sake, don't misunderstand me, misjudge me, mistreat me, and misrepresent me. You see you have missed me four times now, and it makes me feel a little "shaky" about your loving me. You see, friend, when we love a fellow, we can hit him with a hearty handshake and a loving smile, and a kind word and a great big fat "God bless you," and a tender sympathizing, "I am praying for you, old boy." You see love don't know how to misuse a fellow, and the very fact, my friend, that you can keep on missing me, will finally make me feel like you don't love me at all, and, of course, I would hate to feel that way about it.

The first two chapters of the Bible describe a beautiful world with a beautiful garden in it and a man and his wife living in the garden, holy and happy and free from sin, living there in a beautiful world with no sin in it at all; but in the third chapter we see man committing sin, and breaking with God, and fleeing from the presence of God, and then for the next 1,187 chapters we see man fleeing and God pursuing, and in the last two chapters of the Bible we find that God has overtaken man, and they are reconciled, and God has destroyed sin in man and on the earth. Now we see a new heaven and a new earth wherein dwelleth righteousness, and we see holy men and women living in a beautiful world with no sin in it at all, and if we only had the two first and the two last chapters of the Bible we would see a world with holy, happy people in it, and no sin in it.

* * * *

God's best advertisement in this country is a "walking daily," or a "daily walker." In fact, He advertises in no other journal. The Lord's advertisements nowadays are not gotten out on paper and stone with ink and chisel, but they are hung up in smiling faces, kind words, warm handshakes, a twinkle in the eye, a cup of cold water, a warm supper, a little change, a fervent prayer, a pleasant visit, a loving good-bye, a hearty "Come again," an earnest "Don't stay away so long," and, "Please come oftener."

* * * *

J. C. McClure said that "endurance is more effective than brilliancy." He probably had no idea of the wonderful truth he had found, but his statement will live forever. It is almost like inspiration. Brilliancy cannot abide; it is like the passing cloud— it is perfectly beautiful while it lasts, but it is soon forgotten; but not so with endurance. Endurance is that something that you can build on for two worlds and have rock ribs under your feet to stand on.

"Faithful is he that calleth you, who also will do it." Will do what? Well, let us see. He, the Lamb of God that taketh away the sin of the world, will justify me, and He will sanctify me, and He will satisfy me, and He will electrify me, and He will edify me, and He never did horrify me, and some sweet day He will glorify me, and then what? Why, heaven of course, and then what? Why, just more of the same kind of heaven. When we talk of heaven, we really mean a place free from sin and the devil, where there is no sin, and where Jesus is, it is heaven there. When St. Peter got a glimpse of the glorified Christ on the Mount of Transfiguration, he said, "Let us build here three tabernacles, one for Thee, one for Moses and one for Elias." That was as good a heaven as St. Peter wanted; a glorified Christ to look at.

* * * *

The word *church-member* may mean that you have only been born once, but the word *Christian* means that you have been born twice, for it is a fact that you have to be born of the flesh to be a member of the human family, and it is also a fact that you have to be born over again to be a member of the heavenly family. But someone will say, "How can these things be?" Well, reader, that is the same question that was asked by a master in Israel, and that is also the problem that the great theologians of all the ages have hung their heads on and left them hanging there like a hat on the rack, but nevertheless the old Book says to him that believeth all things are possible, and if any man will do My will, he shall know of the doctrine; and, reader, if you have not struck water yet, keep on digging—there is a stream just below you.

* * * *

The saloon is the only factory in existence that is ashamed of its goods after they are manufactured. All the great factories of this country hang a piece of their goods up at the front door of the factory to let the world see what kind of goods they are manufacturing. If the saloonists are not ashamed of their goods, why don't they take a man with a big stomach, a bloated face, a big neck, a red nose, bleared eyes, rundown shoes, greasy breeches, a worn out shirt, a cigar stump in his mouth, a hat on about three numbers too small for him, and hang him up in front of the saloon, and hang a placard to his feet and put in flaming letters on the card, "Run here everybody and see what we are doing." Now, if the saloon was an honest institution, it would do that.

* * * *

The way to make saints is to take equal parts of grace and manhood and mix them together. Grace without man can't make a saint, and man without grace can't make a saint. Therefore, grace and man mixed together is the way saints are made. Well, glory to Jesus! If He will furnish the grace, I will put all the man there is in me into the bowl of consecration and let my Lord do the mixing. Hallelujah!

* * * *

When I was seeking the blessing of sanctification, I thought it would take all the power in heaven to make my heart clean and to satisfy the hunger in my soul, and I told the Lord He could never satisfy me by opening a window in heaven, but let me tell you, folks, about the time the Lord seemed to pass through the cornfield and leave a few smiles hanging up on the corn tassels and I couldn't walk for three hours; and fifteen years have rolled by, and I haven't gotten over it yet. I didn't know how small I was and how great God was. It don't take much of God to fill man to overflowing.

* * * *

I am a drummer for the Human Creator and the World's Manufacturing Association. This is the oldest and most reliable firm in existence. It will be money to you to deal with my company. They honor every order we send in, and send the goods by lightning express with the charges prepaid. Our company is located in the New Jerusalem. We have no competitors; we do business the year round. Why listen longer to the fakirs? They have swindled you out of your money and your manhood and they will swindle you out of your soul next. Come on, and give us your order. You need not put in any money at all until after you receive the goods. My company can put a shine on your face, and if you will walk according to the directions of the company, you will not have to be reshined in a million years.

*   *   *   *

If I wanted to disgrace the devil and put a blotch on the pit and start a scandal through the channels of eternal despair, I would go down into the lower region and get up a rummage sale, such as is gotten up and run by some of the modern churches of our times. Nothing has ever entered into that black country that is as low down as a modern rummage sale. They gather up old dresses, old breeches, old hats and shoes and take them to the church of the Son of God and sell them to the highest bidder to get a little money for the dear Lord. It is a blotch on manhood and womanhood that they will never outgrow in this world or the next. If I were a church member, and a Methodist at that, I would not have Jesus Christ to come in the clouds and catch me at a rummage sale auctioneering off an old pair of dirty breeches for a world like the one we live in. How it must grieve His pure heart!

*   *   *   *

There is not a church on earth strong enough spiritually, financially or socially to support a church kitchen and an amen corner at the same time. When the kitchen comes in at the door the amens go out at the window. They won't work together. Just why they won't work together is not so easy an answer as to ask, but we see there is no affiliation between them. The church kitchen has about the same effect on an amen corner that a snow storm has on a flock of wild geese; when the snow strikes them,

— 46 —

they start for a warmer climate and you hear their sad, sweet song as they pass over you going to a warm south land, and how sad to hear the old saints talk of the good old days long, long ago. What a sad day for the church when she exchanged her amen corner for a kitchen.

*　*　*　*

Almost saved, but yet lost was Judas Iscariot; almost lost, but yet saved was the dying thief; the last act of Judas was to commit suicide; his last words were, "I have betrayed innocent blood," the last words of the dying thief were, "Lord, remember me when thou comest into thy kingdom." What joy and comfort settles down over my soul as I think of those last words, "Lord, remember me when thou comest into thy kingdom," and then thank God. We can sing:

> "The dying thief rejoiced to see
>   That fountain in his day;
> And there may I, though vile as he,
>   Wash all my sins away."

Oh! the contrast between Judas and the thief. Judas was a preacher of the gospel and an apostle of Jesus Christ, chosen by Him, ordained by Him, commissioned by Him and sent forth by Him; a preacher and a thief both dying at the same hour of the day and the preacher lost forever and the thief saved forever; almost saved but lost, and almost lost, but saved. Judas had walked and talked with the Son of God for three years. He was with Him on Galilee when He rebuked the wind and it obeyed Him. He was with Him on the mountainside when He blessed five loaves and two small fishes and fed five thousand men, besides women and children. In fact, Judas had seen all of the wonderful miracles of Jesus and heard Him preach His own everlasting gospel for three years, and was a preacher himself for three years, and the probabilities are that the thief never met Jesus until the day of their crucifixion.

I am persuaded that the thief never had the pleasure of shaking hands with the Son of God, and I am of the opinion that the thief never saw the Son of God until the day of his death, and they were nailed to a Roman cross and hung up to die a few feet apart. The poor thief could not so much as reach out his hand, for it was nailed to the cross, but, thank God, he could look, and I see him turn his face toward the Son of God, and at the same time I see Jesus looking toward him, and their eyes meet probably for the first time in their lives; one a Saviour, the other a sinner; and there they hang and gaze at each other; the sinner remembers all his sins and guilt, the Saviour knows He hath power to blot out all his sins; the sinner knows that he is guilty, the Saviour knows that the thief is lost.

Now the sinner begins to confess, and says, "I am guilty, and I am receiving my just deserts," and he looks at the Saviour, and the Son of God did not look guilty, and the thief knew that the Son of God did not look like he felt, and no doubt but the thief had heard of Him and His wonderful works, and now his eyes behold Him for the first time, and as he hangs there on the cross in agony, both of body and soul, he wonders if the Son of God could do anything for him. Just now he had the opportunity of life, and that was to defend the Son of God in His presence. Now, the other thief that was dying on the other side of Christ and the mob at the foot of the cross, commenced to rail on the Son of God, and this young man, the Bible tells us, took sides with Jesus. Oh, I am so glad he did! and he hurled back into the face of the mob and the other thief, "We are guilty, we are guilty, but this man," referring to Jesus, "hath done nothing wrong or worthy of death." He now turns and looks again at the Son of God and says, "Lord, when thou comest into thy kingdom, remember me," and just about that time the Son of God says to him, "Today, thou shalt be with me in paradise."

Judas Iscariot with the rope around his neck, and the other end to the limb of an olive tree, says, "Farewell, to everything on earth that is dear to me, I have betrayed innocent blood," and he leaps from the limb of the olive tree on the edge of the rock, the rope breaks, he falls over the awful precipice of two worlds at one leap; this world, and the world to come; and, just as he struck the bottom his bowels gushed out and the demons leaped for his lost soul.

The thief on the cross had breathed his last breath and poor Judas went down with an awful crash, and the dying thief went up with the shouts of the angels; almost lost, but altogether saved; almost saved, and yet altogether lost. How sad is thy fate! Oh, lost soul! Would to God I could do something to save thee from the awful horror that hangs around the second death. I warn thee in the name of God the Father, and in the name of Jesus Christ, and in the name of the blessed Holy Ghost, and in the name of the prophets of old. "Turn ye, turn ye, for why will ye die?"

A Few Sign Boards, From Earth to Heaven

We leave the kingdom of sin and darkness, and climb up to the top of Mount Sinai, and there we receive the law. The law reveals to us that we are guilty and condemned, and a hand of fire writes across our conscience the exceeding sinfulness of sin, and with a load of condemnation on us, we make our way from Mount Sinai to Mount Calvary, and there we see One on the cross bleeding and dying for the guilty and condemned, and the load of guilt that we brought from Mount Sinai is unloaded at the foot of the cross on Mount Calvary. The sweet peace of pardon steals its way down into our hearts as we get a glimpse of Him on the tree. We make our way from Mount Calvary to Mount Sion and here we receive the baptism with the Holy Ghost and we are cleansed and made holy and endued with power from on high. From Mount Sinai we make our way to the Mount of Transfiguration, and there we see the glorified Christ. From the Mount of Transfiguration we go to the Mount of Olives, and there we behold the glorified Christ going back to the right hand of the Father; and, as He rides off on the clouds, he says, "I go to prepare a place for you. And if I go and prepare a place for you, I will come again, and will receive you unto myself; that where I am, there ye may be also."

The reader will notice that we go to Mount Sinai for conviction; and we go to Mount Calvary for pardon; and we go to Mount Sion for purity; and we go to the Mount of Transfiguration to get a glimpse of the glorified Christ; and we go to Mount Olivet to behold the ascension. How beautifully these mountain top experiences harmonize with each other and how blessed the thought to the man that stands on Mount Olivet to hear the angel say, "Ye men of Galilee, why stand ye gazing up into heaven? this same Jesus, which is taken up from you into heaven, shall so come in like manner as ye have seen him go into heaven." Just as ye saw Him go up, so shall ye see Him coming back to earth again. Even so, come, Lord Jesus. Amen.

The Great Events of the Bible Took Place on the Mountains

After the flood, the ark rested on the top of a mountain and Noah built an altar unto the Lord and worshiped God under the first rainbow the world ever saw. Abraham offered up Isaac on a mountain. God appeared to Moses in a burning bush on the mount of God. The Lord gave the law and commandments to Moses from the top of Mount Sinai. The first tabernacle was erected on a mountain. Moses went to heaven from the top of Mount Nebo. Elijah proved God to be the true God on Mount Carmel in the presence of eight hundred and fifty false prophets. King Saul, the first king of the children of Israel, took his own life on Mt. Gilboa. The greatest sermon that was ever preached, was preached by Jesus Christ on a mountain. The night before Jesus Christ chose His disciples, He spent the night in prayer on a mountain. Jesus was transfigured before Peter, James and John on a mountain. Jesus Christ was crucified on a mountain. Jesus, after He was resurrected, gave the commission to the disciples to go into the world and preach the gospel to every creature from the top of a mountain in Galilee. Jesus Christ went back to the right hand of the Father from the top of Mount Olivet. These great events are only a part of the things that took place on a mountain, and the meaning of these great events is that you and I are to have a mountain top experience.

Our Kings, Whom Our Souls Delight in, We Will Follow Him

"Behold! a king shall reign in righteousness, and princes shall rule in judgment" Isaiah 32:1. "Thine eyes shall see the king in his beauty: they shall behold the land that is very far off" Isaiah 33:17. "My heart is inditing a good matter: I speak of the things which I have made touching the king: my tongue is the pen of a ready writer" Psalm 45:1. "Behold, the days come, saith the Lord, that I will raise unto David a righteous Branch, and a King shall reign and prosper, and shall execute judgment and justice in the earth" Jer. 23:5. "Afterward shall the children of Israel return, and seek the Lord their God, and David their king; and shall fear the Lord and his goodness in the latter days" Hosea 3:5. "Rejoice greatly, O daughter of Zion; shout, O daughter of Jerusalem: behold, thy King cometh unto thee: he is just, and having salvation; lowly, and riding upon an ass, and upon a colt the foal of an ass. And I will cut off the chariot from Ephraim, and the horse from Jerusalem, and the battle bow shall be cut off: and he shall speak peace unto the heathen: and his dominion shall be from sea even to sea, and from the river even to the ends of the earth" Zech. 9:9, 10.

"And they brought him to Jesus: and they cast their garments upon the colt, and they set Jesus thereon. And, as he went, they spread their clothes in the way. And when he was come nigh, even now at the descent of the mount of Olives, the whole multitude of the disciples began to rejoice and praise God with a loud voice for all the mighty works that they had seen; Saying, Blessed be the King that cometh in the name of the Lord: peace in heaven, and glory in the highest" Luke 19:35-38.

Star Dust is very entertaining, but never effective; it tickles the ear as it falls from the beautiful blue dome, but it never reaches the heart; it creates a smile on the face, but it never brings a tear from the eye; it opens the mouth wide with laughter, but it always shuts the mouth in the testimony meetings; it fills the pews, but it empties the altar; it creates great applause, but it never reports any professions; and yet the star shakers are in great demand. No conference, or association, or synod has ever been able to supply all the pulpits with a star shaker that had put in a call for them. The man that can pitch his tent between Jupiter and Venus, and hang a silk hat on the seven stars, and put his collar and tie on a flying meteor, and prance up and down the Milky Way with a gold cane in his hand, and shave the man in the moon, and cut off his hair and turn somersaults in the Big Dipper; and make a total eclipse in his church on the first Sunday of each month, and make a new moon on the second Sunday, and a full moon on the third and fourth Sundays of each month, is in great demand, and is said to be the greatest preacher of the age. The great churches of our land are bidding on the learned doctor. He is said to be brilliant, and marvelous, and wonderful, and powerful, and the men with gold rings and walking canes, and the women with earrings and lap dogs go wild over the star shaker; and, by the great bulk of church members he is looked on as a great success, when it may be possible that the learned doctor never saw a soul converted under his own ministry in his life, and will stand at the judgment bar of God an empty blank. I have, in the light of God's Word, looked at the doctor from every side carefully with a heart full of love for him; and the only thing that I found that was great about him was found in the fact that he works a great distance from the planet on which he lives; and our great need now is men to work in North America and not on the star. We want 10,000 Spirit-filled men to scratch sand and shovel gravel. Who will volunteer?

A full salvation on a rock foundation is what we want to shout all over this nation. "For their rock is not as our Rock, even our enemies themselves being judges" Deut. 32:31. For St. Peter says, "To whom coming, as unto a living stone, disallowed indeed of men, but chosen of God, and precious. Ye also, as lively stones, are built up a spiritual house, an holy priesthood, to offer up spiritual sacrifices, acceptable to God by Jesus Christ. Wherefore also it is contained in the scripture, Behold, I lay in Sion a chief corner stone, elect, precious: and he that believeth on him shall not be confounded. Unto you therefore which believe he is precious: but unto them which be disobedient, the stone which the builders disallowed, the same is made the head of the corner, and a stone of stumbling, and rock of offence, even to them which stumble at the word, being disobedient: whereunto also they were appointed. But ye are a chosen generation, a royal priesthood, an holy nation, a peculiar people; that ye should shew forth the praises of him who hath called you out of darkness into his marvelous light" I Peter 2:4-9. "And I say also unto thee, That thou art Peter, and upon this rock I will build my church and the gates of hell shall not prevail against it" Matt. 16:18.

"Wherefore? Because they sought it not by faith, but as it were by the works of the law. For they stumbled at that stumblingstone; as it is written, Behold, I lay in Sion a stumblingstone and rock of offence: and whosoever believeth in him shall not be ashamed" Rom. 9:32, 33. "Behold I will stand before thee there upon the rock in Horeb; and thou shalt smite the rock, and there shall come water out of it, that the people may drink. And Moses did so in the sight of the elders of Israel" Ex. 17:6. "And Moses took the rod from before the Lord, as he commanded him. And Moses and Aaron gathered the congregation together before the rock; and he said unto them, Hear now, ye rebels, must we fetch you water out of this rock? And Moses lifted up his hand, and with his rod he smote the rock twice: and the water came out abundantly, and the congregation drank, and their beasts also" Num. 20:9, 10, 11. "And he said, The Lord is my rock, and my fortress, and my deliverer; the God of my rock; in him will I trust: he is my shield, and the horn of my salvation, my high tower, and my refuge, my Saviour; thou savest me from violence" II Sam. 22:2, 3.

Moses wants to see God's glory. "And he said, I beseech thee, shew me thy glory. And he said, I will make all my goodness pass before thee, and I will proclaim the name of the Lord before thee; and will be gracious to whom I will be gracious, and will show mercy on whom I will shew mercy. And he said, Thou canst not see my face: for there shall no man see me, and live. And the Lord said, Behold, there is a place by me, and thou shalt stand upon a rock: And it shall come to pass, while my glory passeth by, that I will put thee in a cleft of the rock, and will cover thee with my hand while I pass by: And I will take away mine hand, and thou shalt see my back parts: but my face shall not be seen" Ex. 33:18-23.

"Who led thee through that great and terrible wilderness, wherein were fiery serpents, and scorpions, and drought, where there was no water; who brought thee forth water out of the rock of flint; who fed thee in the wilderness with manna, which thy fathers knew not, that he might humble thee, and that he might prove thee, to do thee good at thy latter end" Deut. 8:15, 16. "He is the Rock, his work is perfect: for all his ways are judgment: a God of truth and without iniquity, just and right is he" Deut. 32:4. "There is none holy as the Lord; for there is none beside thee: neither is there any rock like our God" I Sam. 2:2.

"As for God, his way is perfect; the word of the Lord is tried: he is a buckler to all them that trust in him. For who is God, save the Lord? and who is a rock, save our God? The Lord liveth; and blessed be my rock; and exalted be the God of the rock of my salvation" II Sam. 22:31, 32, 47. "The God of Israel said, the Rock of Israel spake to me, He that ruleth over men must be just, ruling in the fear of God" II Sam. 23:3.

"And he said, Go forth, and stand upon the mount before the Lord. And, behold, the Lord passed by, and a great and strong wind rent the mountains, and brake in pieces the rocks before the Lord; but the Lord was not in the wind: and after the wind an earthquake; but the Lord was not in the earthquake: And after the earthquake a fire; but the Lord was not in the fire: and after the fire a still small voice. And it was so, when Elijah heard it, that he wrapped his face in his mantle, and went out, and stood in the entering in of the cave. And, behold, there came a voice unto him, and said, What doest thou here, Elijah?"

"For in the time of trouble he shall hide me in his pavilion: in the secret of his tabernacle shall he hide me; he shall set me up upon a rock" Psalm 27:5. "For thou art my rock and my fortress; therefore for thy name's sake lead me, and guide me" Psalm 31:3.

"He brought me up also out of an horrible pit, out of the miry clay, and set my feet upon a rock, and established my goings" Psalm 40:2. "From the end of the earth will I cry unto thee, when my heart is overwhelmed: lead me to the rock that is higher than I" Psalm 61:2. "Be thou my strong habitation, whereunto I may continually resort: thou hast given commandment to save me; for thou art my rock and my fortress" Psalm 71:3. "I will set his hand also in the sea, and his right hand in the rivers. He shall cry unto me, Thou art my father, my God and the rock of my salvation. Also I will make him my firstborn, higher than the kings of the earth. My mercy will I keep for him forevermore, and my covenant shall stand fast with him" Psalm 89:25, 26, 27, 28.

"O come, let us sing unto the Lord: let us make a joyful noise to the rock of our salvation" Psalm 95:1. "The righteous shall flourish like the palm tree: he shall grow like a cedar in Lebanon. Those that be planted in the house of the Lord shall flourish in the courts of our God. They shall still bring forth fruit in old age; they shall be fat and flourishing; To shew that the Lord is upright: he is my rock, and there is no unrighteousness in him" Psalm 92:12-15.

"O my dove, that art in the clefts of the rock, in the secret places of the stairs, let me see thy countenance, let me hear thy voice; for sweet is thy voice, and thy countenance is comely" Sol. 2:14. "Because thou hast forgotten the God of thy salvation, and hast not been mindful of the rock of thy strength, therefore shalt thou plant pleasant plants, and shalt set it with strange slips" Isaiah 17:10. "And a man shall be as an hiding place from the wind, and a covert from the tempest; as rivers of water in a dry place, as the shadow of a great rock in a weary land" Isaiah 32:2. "Is not my word like as a fire? saith the Lord; and like a hammer that breaketh the rock in pieces?" Jer. 23:29.

"Therefore whosoever heareth these sayings of mine, and doeth them, I will liken him unto a wise man, which built his house upon a rock: And the rain descended, and the floods came, and the winds blew, and beat upon that house; and it fell not: for it was founded upon a rock" Matt. 7:24, 25. "Moreover, brethren, I would not that ye should be ignorant, how that all our fathers were under the cloud, and all passed through the sea; And were all baptized unto Moses in the cloud and in the sea; And did all eat the same spiritual meat; And did all drink the same spiritual drink: for they drank of that spiritual Rock that followed them: and that Rock was Christ" I Cor. 10:1-4.

"Whosoever cometh to me, and heareth my sayings, and doeth them, I will shew you to whom he is like: He is like a man which built an house, and digged deep, and laid the foundation on a rock: and when the flood arose, the stream beat vehemently upon that house, and could not shake it: for it was founded upon a rock" Luke 6:47, 48.

What Is a Good Religious Experience?

Why, a good religious experience means that I was convicted for my sins, and that I repented of my sins, and confessed my sins, and forsook my sins, and that God pardoned my sins, and gave me the witness of the Spirit that my sins were blotted out, and that my name was written in heaven, and that I was a son of God, and that I had been adopted into the heavenly family, and that now I was an heir to the baptism with the Holy Ghost and fire, and that God would sanctify me wholly and preserve me blameless unto the coming of the Lord Jesus Christ; and that I could graze in the red top clover field where the bees make honey all the year, and where the hummingbirds sing their sweet humming melody all the year, and buzz in the honeysuckle vines, as they climb the tree of life that hath been planted in my soul, and that out in the backyard of my soul I have a half-dozen old bee gums that I have not robbed yet this year, and it means that you are so filled with God, that sin, in any form, is so disgusting to you, that the devil can't get up anything to attract you at all. You are just simply lost in the ocean of God's love; and you are just floating about in divine grace and expecting to float to the eternal city in a short time; and that if you were to make the landing today, you would not be surprised at all; and that you are a stranger and a pilgrim here on earth; and that here you "have no continuing city, but you seek one to come whose builder and maker is God"; and that the hard places in life are just stepping stones to greater blessings in this world; and that when you meet with what the devil calls an impossibility, you just take the handspike of faith, and turn the thing over, and find an oil well, and a gold mine, and a flitter tree, and a honey pond, and the river of life all there under what the devil wanted you to see as an impossibility.

When the devil brings you up to what he calls a surrounding circumstance, you just put the saddle of faith on him, and ride him to the city of success and hitch him up to the post of industry, and pray down an old-time revival that will cause men to run across Jordan, shout down Jericho, kill Achan and march up and take Ai; and when the devil brings up what he calls a great difficulty, just take the key of faith, and unlock his doors and go into his inward treasures, and you will find something like an old-fashioned Tennessee cupboard with the shelves loaded down with grapes and pomegranates, milk and honey, and you will have nothing to do but to eat and shine and shout and praise God from whom all blessings flow. Now that is what I call a good religious experience.

The Best Place on Earth

Where is it? Well, now, just come with me and I will show you the man that has God for his Father; Jesus Christ for his Saviour, the Holy Ghost for his Abiding Comforter, and his heart full of grace, heaven in his eye, glory all over his soul, a spring in his heel, oil on his face, and a determination to go through in spite of the devil and his adversaries; with his back turned to this old world, his face turned toward heaven, and walking all day with God the Father, going to sleep at night in the arms of Jesus Christ, dreaming of the eternal city and its inhabitants, and waking up in the morning and looking out over the hills of the earth, and watching the sun rise, washing his face off in the blue sky, and wiping on the clouds of heaven, that man is evidently in the best place on earth.

The saddest thing I have ever seen, since I saw the first thing I ever saw, was a man with white hair and a black heart, a wrinkled face and a dead soul; with vengeance on his brow, and murder in his bosom, with no joy, but a heap of trouble, with no peace, but a great quantity of unrest and dissatisfaction, with no love, but filled with hatred, with no friends, but plenty of enemies, with no light, but filled with darkness, with no grace, but loaded down to the water-line with sin, with no money to buy food, but an appetite for strong drink, driving him to the grog shop like a beast to the slaughter pen, with no salvation, but with damnation already burning in his very bones, with no Christ to love and pity him, but with bloated-faced devils to mock and hiss at him, as he washes out spittoons in the back alleys of your city, for a morning eye-opener, with no heaven in sight, but an awful hell of eternal misery just waiting for him to stagger and fall under his load of guilt and condemnation and plunge into outer darkness, where the worm dieth not and the fire is not quenched.

Now, reader, I want it to be understood once for all that there is no such a thing as a happy old sinner in existence now, and never was, and never will be, you may take the back track of the human family and go back to the birthday of Adam and then come back and take the lightning express and go on down the stream of time until you meet the Son of God coming in the clouds of heaven and you will find that after you have examined the past, present and future that such a thing as a happy old sinner was never heard of in any age of the world. The devil hasn't got any happy old sinners and never has had one; and, of course, he never will have, for such a thing is unscriptural, unreasonable and impossible. The man that goes through this world a God-forgetter, a Christ-despiser and a blood-rejecter has opened his gates to the fowls of the air, and the beasts of the field and the fowls of this world will flop their black skinny wings in his face and sting his guilty conscience like a bald headed hornet, and the beasts of the field will get on his track and run him to the places of shame where wretchedness, misery and woe will settle down over his soul like an awful nightmare, and like Cain of old, he will be heard to cry out, "My misery is greater than I can bear." As truly as Cain went through this world a marked man, the man that says "no" to God and "yes" to the devil will go through this world with a mark on him that cannot be covered up; for there he stands now on the street corner with a bloated stomach, a big neck, a swollen face with bleared eyes and a red nose. Marked! Marked! Marked! Of course he is marked and branded, and there is no devil in hell or on earth but what would recognize him as one of their samples; and there he stands on the street corner on exhibition. You can see him any day in the week, but, alas! my brother, in a few days you will leave a mocking, hissing, sin-cursed, devil-ridden world, and go to meet an offended God who will drive you from His judgment bar, and you will go out into outer darkness and you will meet a herd of croaking devils where you are to spend an awful eternity. My God! sinner, I have followed you through a life of sin until my poor heart is ready to scream, and I throw myself across the road to hell and wave a red lantern across your path and cry from the depths of my soul, "O man, why will ye die! why will ye die! In the name of God the Father I warn you of hell, and in the name of Jesus Christ I warn you of hell! Why will ye die! Why will ye die!"

We have been on the track of the old sinner for a few minutes. Now, come with me and let us look at the old saint for a little while. I think the loveliest sight I ever saw was an old man eighty-eight years old on a platform in the presence of fifteen hundred people, with glory in his soul, and heaven hung up all over his face, and, as he leaped and praised God and his snow white locks floated in the air, I sat and watched him, and it seemed to me that you could have taken a hand towel and wiped enough heaven off of his face to have saved every sinner in the town, if they had only said "yes" to God. While this old saint leaped and praised God on the platform, his old wife, who was eighty-five years old, could not stand it any longer and she leaped from her seat and spun around on her feet like a fifteen-year-old school girl, and clapped her hands and shouted, "Glory to God! I am feeling just like John is acting." John was her husband. The preacher in charge saw the situation and just sat back and looked on and let these two white-haired children run the thing, and I am here to tell you there was not anything left out that goes in to make up a religious meeting.

After the old saint had leaped and praised God for at least twenty minutes, he faced that great throng of people, and his old white face literally gleamed with the presence of God, and he shouted to the top of his voice, "Say, then people, God is here, do you want Him? If so, come this way." Men and women ran down the aisles and climbed over benches and tumbled over themselves to get to the altar. I watched how easy it was to get them to the altar, and then remembered I the word of the Lord, "If I be lifted up I will draw all men unto me." That man did not need a song, or to coax folks, to get them to move. The only trouble he had was in having a place large enough to hold the crowd that went forward for prayers. After all, my friend, this old world wants to see God, and the man that can show the hungry world the Christ of Calvary will have no trouble in getting people to an altar for prayer. The old man on the platform had God on exhibition, or the Lord had him there. It was hard to tell which was on the throne, the Lord or the saint. As I write there comes to my mind an old saint, a mother in Israel. I remember her now as I last saw her. She was on a platform in the presence of three or four thousand people leading the testimony meeting, and she was close to ninety-five years old. As she listened to the testimonies she finally got to the place where she could not control herself and she shouted off her spectacles and cap, and her old face looked more like the face of an angel than the face of a woman. While that old saint literally pranced up and down on that big platform, the great mass of people almost went wild and she seemed to be as light and active as a sixteen-year-old girl.

Now reader, the devil has no ninety-five-year-old sinner that ever got happy and shouted. We must turn to the righteous to find happy old people, for there is not one to be found on the other side.

Well, bless the Lord, there are some things about the religion of Jesus Christ that are not found in anything else. The religion of Jesus Christ makes old people happy, and the nearer they come to the grave, the greater their joy. They are the only crowd that walk on earth that can truly say from their hearts, "O death, where is thy string? O grave, where is thy victory?" For the old saint Jesus Christ has captured death and pulled his stinger out, and He has made the grave a stepping stone to the eternal city, and the things that look as dark as midnight to the old sinner look as bright as heaven to the old saint, and he can see clear through and see his own face in the looking glass on the shelves in the parlors of glory, and it prepares him for all the conflicts of life, and he knows that he will be more than conqueror through Him that loved him, and gave Himself for him. Therefore, he never goes to battle with any expectation of defeat. He knows he will come off the battlefield victorious. Therefore, he goes out singing Holiness unto the Lord now and forever. The old saint that can reach up and take hold of Jesus Christ can defeat the devil on any part of the battlefield and not use up one-half of his ammunition, and I am praising God for the fact that anything that is good for an old saint has a fine effect on a younger one. As they pass over, we are prepared to take their place and go on with the work where they laid it down. If they conquered, we can; and we know they did, for we saw them, and they looked like angels when they were overcoming the devil by "the blood of the Lamb, and the word of their testimony"; and they loved not their lives unto death, but were strong in the faith, giving glory to God, being fully persuaded that what God has promised He is able to perform. Therefore, they staggered not through unbelief, but kept their eye on Him, who never lost a battle, and He brought them out from thence that He might bring them into the land that He sware to their fathers to give them for an inheritance.

Well, amen, thank God, we see them passing over Jordan every day and getting into their delightsome land.

A Preacher of the Gospel of Jesus Christ

What is he anyhow? In the first place, he is a man called of God; in the second place, he is a man commissioned of God; and in the third place, he is a man sent of God. So now we have a man God-called, God-commissioned, and God-sent. We have that much sure. He must be that to be a preacher at all, and he is ready to go out at God's call, not knowing whither he goeth. There are a few things he must know and be in possession of to be a successful minister of the Lord Jesus Christ. He must know God the Father, God the Son and God the Holy Ghost. He must know God as his Father, Jesus Christ as his Saviour and Sanctifier, and the blessed Holy Ghost as his Abiding Comforter, and then he will know that the redeemed saints of all the ages are his brothers and sisters, and that the angels are his companions, and that heaven is his eternal home, and when these things take place in his life, he will have a religious experience as deep as the demand of fallen humanity, as broad as the compassion of God, as high as heaven, and as everlasting as the Rock of Ages. He will see something in every poor sinner on earth that is worth sacrificing his life for, and he will not love his life unto death, for he is a whole burnt offering, or a living sacrifice; in other words, he is an empty channel for God to pour grace through, or in other words, he is a blank for God to write anything on that He wishes to write, and he stands by the roadside like a billboard and God writes just what He wants the people to read.

You see, brother, the man that puts up a billboard never consults the board as to what he puts it on, neither does the Lord consult his servant. He gives the message, and the God-sent man delivers it just as was delivered to him; he neither adds to nor takes from it. If it is a message of love, he delivers it in the name of his Master; if it is a message on hell, he delivers it in fear and trembling, leaving the results with the God who sent the message, for a God-sent man must be a man of obedience, and he must be clean inside and outside, blood-red, sky-blue, and snow-white, a walking flame of fire, a living monument, a standing rebuke to a non-believing world, and a half-believing church. He must be a cyclone of grace and glory to succeed in this world, and rescue the perishing. The preacher is a failure that is only keeping the pews together that his father put together. He must get new pews to add to the building, or the old building will soon tumble and leave him without a job. So then a God-sent man must be as bold as a lion; he neither fears men nor devils. He has a backbone as big as a sawlog. In fact, God Himself is the backbone of the God-sent man. He can clean up the devil on any part of the field and not use half of his ammunition, for he is charged and surcharged with the God of the universe, and therefore, he stands by the word of truth as bold as a lion. He knows nothing of rounding off the corners, or apologizing for the truth as he finds it in the blessed Old Book. If he is waited on by the official board, as they sometimes are, for preaching so straight, he informs them that they are too late, that he got the message from headquarters. A God-sent man is as patient as an ox, he will pull a day or a year as the case may be. Wherever the Lord hitches up a fellow and puts him to pulling, there he pulls till the Lord sends him elsewhere. He will pull all day and on till midnight at anything he is hitched to, and then lie down by it at night and go to sleep chewing his cud. He is delivered from fret and worry; he is long-suffering, plenteous in mercy, and slow to anger. He is patient with both his friends and his enemies, for he knows he will succeed in spite of all his adversaries, and come off more than conqueror through Him that loved him and gave Himself for him, that He might redeem him from all iniquity and purify unto Himself a peculiar man zealous of good works; therefore, he "endures as seeing him who is invisible"; nothing in his way, everything he meets with is a stepping stone to something higher or better. A God-called man is as swift as an eagle.

He just touches the earth in the highest places; he is not entangled with the affairs of this world; he lives in heaven and walks on the earth; he sets his nest on high and when trials, hardships, misunderstandings, misrepresentations, mistreatment, misjudgments, and the darts from the enemies' bow fall thick and fast, he sits down on the Rock of Ages and rests from all his enemies, and finally goes to sleep in the arms of Jesus, while the angels fan him with the breezes of heaven and he dreams of climbing the tree of life with the blood-washed spirits in that beautiful land of delight. When he wakes up, he can take to his spiritual wings and sail out in the blue skies of God's love and look down on death and destruction and feel no harm from fiery darts of the enemy's bow.

Glory to God, I feel like I am flying now. Hallelujah for the Lamb that was slain! Who hath loved us and washed us from our sins in His own blood, and made us kings and priests unto God forever and ever! Amen and Amen.

A God-called man is as wise as a serpent; he goes where he ought to go and stays away from the places where he ought not to be. He stays long enough at any one place, but when the time comes for him to leave, he goes from there. Now don't you catch on? He must shun the very appearance of evil, and in order to do that he must have the wisdom of a serpent. How many preachers have ruined themselves in this world and I fear in the one to come, by hanging around places where they ought not to be? How bad they need the wisdom of a serpent!

Now, reader, if you know anything about a serpent you know that if he thinks there is danger on hand, he is pulling his freight in an opposite direction. He never hangs around just to see how near he can get to danger and then escape, but he tries to see how far he can keep from it.

The preacher that is caught, bound by unscriptural oaths to a secret order, hath not the wisdom of a serpent, but while he slept, his Delilah hath shorn him of his spiritual locks, and he is as weak as burnt tow, and his enemies will gouge out his spiritual eyes and put him in the mills of Dagon to grind and make sport for the Philistines.

Oh, my brother, keep your heart out of such a halter! The enemies will lead you into danger and you will be powerless to resist or to rebuke, and like Samson of old, your worldly association will mock at you, and say, where is your God? They have stolen your gold and left you nothing but brass, and worse still, they have stolen your fire and you have settled down to cold, dead, formal worldliness, and as a preacher you will be toothless, juiceless and powerless, lifeless and dead, and you will grieve year in and year out with no fire on God's altar. There are but two things you will do successfully; one is to draw your breath and the other is like unto it, draw your salary. A preacher with a long coat, white tie, kid gloves, but no God, no Christ, no Holy Ghost, no power, no unction, no fire and no juice, is of all creatures on earth, most to be pitied.

The preachers that have drifted into such places are so blinded by the great mills of Dagon, that they do not even feel the need of love or sympathy; and if you offer them deliverance through the blood of the Crucified Saviour, they will mock at you and grind on. I know some of these intellectual giants that belong to every secret order in the whole land and fill some of the greatest pulpits in the land, and they are great talkers, lovely fellows, and have not seen a soul brought to Christ under their ministry in years, and the sad thought of it all is, they go right on, year in and year out, without a convert, and they are so dead they are not at all alarmed about themselves, or about the church of which they are pastor. They have stoned the flock to death instead of giving them the bread of life.

Now the Bible says: "Feed the flock of God" and another text says, "Feed the church of God which he hath purchased with his own blood." Now again the Bible says, "Preach the word," and Christ says, "My word shall not return unto me void," and He says again, "The heavens and the earth will pass away, but my word shall not pass away."

O thou brother of my soul, be as wise as a serpent, and touch not, taste not, handle not these things that are to perish with their using, but get a grip on God and the things that are eternal with both hands and hold on with a death grip, and die before you will say "yes" to a Godless, Christless, fun-loving world.

We need men; and if you can't do what a man ought to do, we can't use you. We want men. A man that is God-sent will be as gentle as a lamb. A God-sent preacher is a perfect gentleman in every sense of the word. He is loving, gentle, tender and Christ-like, easy to be entreated, not hard to approach, with a listening ear, a tender heart, a forgiving spirit, and is a bundle of sympathy. He knows where to be bold; he knows where to be patient; he knows where to be swift; he knows where to be wise, and he also knows where to be gentle. There are some homes he enters, where he must be a father; he enters other homes where he is to sit and listen and learn of the deep things of God, and there take the place of a little child, for if he is as gentle as a lamb, he is willing to be led where he finds someone that has gone over the ground before him and understands leading the procession.

A God-sent man is as harmless as a dove; there is no harm or danger in a God-sent man. He has a message from God, and in the name and for the glory of his Master, he delivers that message, and it can be said of him as of one of old, "Behold an Israelite indeed in whom is no guile." There is no danger to the family that takes care of the preacher that is as harmless as a dove; but on the other hand, how great a blessing will come to the home of such a family!

You remember the blessing that came to the house of Obed-edom because he took care of the ark of God. Well, a preacher that is as harmless as a dove is nothing more or less than the ark of God walking up and down on the earth. He is just simply an ark on legs. He is just a little tabernacle within himself, and the presence of God is to abide with him continually, and the fire never goes out on the altar of his soul, and the dove of peace sits on the limbs of the tree of life that is planted in his soul, and sings the year in, and then, bless the Lord, sings the year out.

The dove is the most harmless thing, I suppose, that lives on the earth; therefore, Jesus Christ says to His preachers, "Be ye as harmless as doves." Now, if the preacher will obey the words of his Master, he is a safe man. He is a delivered man; he will be a blessing to the world in which he lives. He will build up the church, he will pull down the strong-holds of Satan, and the world in which he lives will never forget him, and will name their children after him after he has been dead hundreds of years.

Well, now reader, the next thought: A God-sent man is as sweet as honey, that is, he hasn't a sour backbone. He has a sweet backbone, and can lift a heavier load and carry it further and hold out longer than the man can with a sour backbone.

The Old Book says, it is as sweet as honey and the honey-comb; another writer in the Old Book says, it was like honey in his mouth for sweetness; and another Bible character came out of the woods with a camel skin thrown across his shoulders and an Old Testament scroll under his arm and his breeches rolled up to his knees, and long shaggy hair down to his shoulders, and a pair of fiery eyes looking through the people, as he met them, and with honey all over his hands, he said to the people, "Repent for the kingdom of heaven is at hand." And they seemed to believe it, for they felt that they were in the presence of a God-sent man.

Now reader, I want to say that when a sinner meets with a God-sent man, he knows him on first sight, and is ready to stack arms, for when a sinner looks a God-sent man in the face there is no strength left in him, and his knees smite one against the other. The reader will pardon me for speaking of myself, but just a few days ago, I saw a great strong looking man, at least six feet high, and would weigh one hundred and eighty pounds, stand in my congregation, and he looked pale and haggard. I walked to him, put my hand on him and he trembled like a leaf in the wind. I said, "Come on, brother, God's eye is on you," and he started and staggered as he came, and by the time he reached the altar, he fell as limber as a rag and cried for God to save his poor lost soul, and bless God, it was not thirty minutes until that man picked me up in his big strong arms and walked off with me, and it seemed that the whole city of the New Jerusalem was hung up in his face; and better still, the sins were gone out of his dear heart, and he had passed from darkness to light, from the power of Satan unto God, from death to life, and from a bond slave of the devil to a free son of God, from a pauper to a millionaire; and he felt that his name was written in heaven. So we see that if a man will keep sweet in his soul, there is no telling what God can do with him, at least, he will be a blessing to the world in which he lives, and not only while he is living, but his life will be a blessing to the rising generation, and people will rise up and call him blessed after he has been in heaven hundreds of years.

I just heard an old preacher blessing God a few days ago for the life of John S. Inskip. He said thirty-two years ago, he went to hear Inskip preach, and before he ever preached a sermon, he called mourners, and that he went to the altar to be sanctified, and was gloriously sanctified and had all the rest of the meeting to shout in. As the old saint blessed God for the life of Inskip, his old face gleamed with a halo of glory, and the big tears chased each other down his wrinkled cheeks. I say, bless God for every good man that ever lived on earth!

Now, dear reader, a God-called, God-commissioned, and God-sent man is bold where he ought to be bold, and patient where he ought to be patient, and swift where he ought to be swift, and wise where he ought to be wise, and is gentle where he ought to be gentle, and is harmless where he ought to be harmless, and is sweet when he ought to be sweet, and that makes up a well-rounded man, or in other words what we call a holiness evangelist, such as H. C. Morrison, B. Carradine, C. J. Fowler, Joseph H. Smith, E. F. Walker, A. M. Hills, or scores of others we could name whose names are in the Book of life.

Well, glory to God! I have salvation all over my soul and grace on both sides of my religious experience. Hallelujah!

The Personality and Divinity of Jesus Christ

Jesus Christ was the only person ever born that was called "the seed of the woman." Everybody else on earth is called the seed of man. Jesus Christ said of Himself that He took on Him, not the nature of angels, but He took on Him the seed of Abraham. So the seed of woman and the seed of Abraham are found in the person of Jesus Christ, and we behold the Babe in the manger in the city of Bethlehem, for the prophet Micah said seven hundred and ten years before Christ was born in; Micah 5:2; "But thou, Bethlehem Ephratah, though thou be little among the thousands of Judah, yet out of thee shall he come forth unto me that is to be ruler in Israel; whose goings forth have been from of old, from everlasting." Now see how the words of the angel in conversation with Mary harmonize with the words of Micah, although Micah had prophesied seven hundred and ten years before the conversation between Mary and the angel. We read in Luke 1:30-33: "And the angel said unto her, Fear not, Mary: for thou hast found favour with God. And, behold, thou shalt conceive in thy womb and bring forth a son, and shalt call his name Jesus. He shall be great and shall be called the Son of the Highest: and the Lord God shall give unto him the throne of his father David: and he shall reign over the house of Jacob forever: and of his kingdom there shall be no end."

We next notice another prophecy in the Old Bible in perfect harmony with the words spoken by the angel concerning the blessed Christ that was born in Bethlehem of Judea, and this prophecy was uttered six hundred and three years before Christ was born. We read in Daniel 2:44-45, "And in the days of these kings shall the God of heaven set up a kingdom, which shall never be destroyed: and the kingdom shall not be left to other people, but it shall break in pieces and consume all these kingdoms, and it shall stand for ever. For as much as thou sawest that the stone was cut out of the mountain without hands, that it brake in pieces the iron, the brass, the clay, the silver and the gold; the great God hath made known to the king what shall come to pass hereafter: and the dream is certain, and the interpretation thereof sure."

The reader will notice that this wonderful dream of Nebuchadnezzar was fulfilled on the night when the angel band swung low in the skies and sang, "Glory to God in the highest, and on earth peace, good will toward men," although six hundred long, weary years had rolled by since the king saw in his wonderful vision, a stone cut out of the mountain without hands, and saw it break in pieces, the iron, the brass, the clay, the silver and the gold, and roll on till it had filled the whole earth and subdued and broken down every kingdom on earth.

Bless God, the rolling stone that filled the earth was none other than the blessed Christ that I met a few years ago in Texas, and salvation broke in on me like a mighty mountain till it filled my heart with grace and glory. Now this blessed One that is spoken of by the prophets to fulfill prophecy had to exchange the New Jerusalem in the skies for the Jerusalem in Palestine. He had to exchange heaven for a stable; He had to exchange His throne in the skies for a bed in the ox trough; He had to put on humanity to enable us to put on divinity; He had to become the son of man to enable us to become the sons and daughters of the Almighty; He had to put on us before we could put on Him; He had to make an awful plunge, for we were on the bottom and nobody but a deep diver could find us and bring us to the top; we were clear down under the mud sill and no use for a shallow diver to look for us. We were sinners by nature and sinners by practice, and a sinner is a being that is just as far from God as a being can be. There is nothing that separates God and man but sin; therefore, sin puts a human soul just as far from God as it can be put, but thank God, Jesus Christ was in this country devising plans by which the sinner that was afar off from God could be brought nigh, for we read in Eph. 2:13, "But now in Christ Jesus ye who sometimes were far off are made nigh by the blood of Christ." So by the blood of Christ the way is opened up for us from darkness to light and from bondage to freedom, and from sin to righteousness, and from death to life and from hell to heaven, and no man need perish, for Christ hath opened up a new and living way for us" Heb. 10:20.

And we see that it took both the divinity and humanity of Jesus Christ to open up for us this new and living way. The apostle says that this new and living way was opened up through His flesh, that is, through the divinity and humanity of Jesus Christ. The middle wall of partition was broken down, not only between the Jew and the Gentile, but between God and man, and now Jesus Christ being both God and man has defeated the devil and broken the power of sin, and put a bridge over hell, and where sin abounded grace did much more abound, and where sin, death and hell reigned, now, thank God, through the man Christ Jesus, life and immortality are brought to light, and we no longer have to walk in darkness, but we have the light of life.

Now, we want to look at a few passages of Scripture that bring out both the humanity and divinity of Jesus Christ. We first notice Him coming to John for baptism. We read in Matthew 3:13-15, "Then cometh Jesus from Galilee to Jordan unto John, to be baptized of him, but John forbad him, saying, I have need to be baptized of thee, and comest thou to me? And Jesus answering said unto him, Suffer it to be so now for thus it becometh us to fulfill all righteousness. Then he suffered him." The very fact that Jesus Christ submitted to water baptism proves His humanity, but we notice now in the first verse of the fourth chapter of Matthew just as soon as John baptized Jesus, "He was led up of the Spirit into the wilderness to be tempted of the devil," and no man can read the fourth chapter of Matthew and see the conflict between Christ and the devil and fail to see the divinity of Jesus Christ. He was baptized like a man, but he defeated the devil like a God. It takes a man to submit to water baptism, but it takes divinity to clean up the devil and put him to flight, and our Christ did both. Bless His holy name! That makes us feel comfortable.

We next notice the Sermon on the Mount recorded in the fifth, sixth and seventh chapters of Matthew's gospel. We see Him climb the hill with His disciples, not with all the people around Jerusalem, but only with a select crowd, and He walks and climbs the mountain, and somewhere up the mountainside He sits down, and we read that "he opened his mouth and taught them, saying," and the message that Jesus Christ delivered to His disciples there on the mountainside challenges the world. The words were more than the words of a man; from the time our gracious heavenly Father walked with Adam in the garden of Eden until this good hour, there never was such a message delivered to any man or any set of men as is recorded in the Sermon on the Mount.

The words that fell from the lips of the Christ there on the mountainside will live when this old world is burned into cinders. I am satisfied in my own mind that there is enough subject matter in each one of the three chapters in the Sermon on the Mount to make a book within itself if each thought expressed in them were properly discussed. He climbed to the mountaintop like a man, but He sat down and taught like a God.

We now read in the eighth chapter of Matthew that, "When he was comedown from the mountain, great multitudes followed him. And, behold, there came a leper and worshiped him, saying, Lord, if thou wilt, thou canst make me clean. And Jesus put forth his hand, and touched him, saying, I will; be thou clean. And immediately his leprosy was cleansed."

This is the first miracle that Matthew records that Jesus performed, and there is one other thought connected with the healing of this leper that I want you to notice. This is the only case on record where the afflicted one threw all the responsibility of his healing back on Jesus Christ. The leper said, "Lord, if thou wilt, thou canst make me clean." And the words had no sooner fallen from his lips than Jesus said, "I will; be thou clean." And the Book says, "Immediately his leprosy was cleansed."

The next thought we want to notice is the healing of the centurion's servant. We read in the eighth chapter of Matthew, "And when Jesus was entered into Capernaum, there came unto him a centurion, beseeching him, and saying, Lord, my servant lieth at home sick of the palsy, grievously tormented. And Jesus saith unto him, I will come and heal him. The centurion answered and said, Lord, I am not worthy that thou shouldest come under my roof; but speak the word only, and my servant shall be healed" Matt. 8:5, 6, 7, 8.

Now, we read that Jesus marvelled at the faith of this centurion, and said, "I have not found so great faith, no, not in Israel." Now when we see Jesus standing on a street corner in Capernaum in conversation with a man, concerning a sick servant, we see Him as man, but when we hear Him speak a word, and, behold, we look and see a man miles away, getting out of his bed, we know that He is more than man, He is a God.

We next notice the healing of Peter's wife's mother in this same chapter; "And when Jesus was come into Peter's house, he saw his wife's mother laid, and sick of a fever. And he touched her hand, and the fever left her: and she arose and ministered unto them." Now the walking down in the streets of Capernaum denotes humanity, but to touch the hand of a sick woman and see her arise is a mark of divinity. When Christ healed this woman, He did not anoint her with oil; He did not call on James and John and Peter to pray. Well, bless His name, what did He do? He touched her hand, and glory to God! she got up and wasn't weak for a week or ten days, but was healed on the spot. I don't think the old lady ever had the fever again. Matthew 8:14, 15.

We notice now in the 16th and 17th verses: "When the even was come, they brought unto him many that were possessed with devils: and he cast out the spirits with his word, and healed all that were sick: That it might be fulfilled which was spoken by Esaias the prophet, saying, Himself took our infirmities, and bare out sicknesses." We have no idea how many people were healed there in that great healing service, for the Book says many, and the word many has no limit. There might have been one hundred, or there might have been a thousand, but thank God, the Word says they were all healed, not one went away unhealed, and Matthew says that when He was doing this healing that He was fulfilling prophecy, not that Christ only wanted to fulfill the words of the prophecy, but it had been prophesied of Him that He would do these things, and the time had come for this prophecy to be fulfilled, and Christ, with a heart overflowing with love for the sick and afflicted, stands at Peter's front door and I believe the streets were blocked, and sick people, and devil-ridden people were standing around Him for fifty feet, and I think some were coming groaning, and others going back shouting; some with an eye out; some on beds carried by friends, but, behold, they all go back healed of their diseases. We read again in this chapter from the twenty-third to the twenty-sixth verse, "And when he was entered into a ship, his disciples followed him, and behold, there arose a great tempest in the sea, insomuch that the ship was covered with the waves: but he was asleep. And his disciples came to him, and awoke him, saying, Lord, save us: we perish. And he saith unto them, Why are ye fearful, O ye of little faith? Then he arose, and rebuked the winds and the sea, and there was a great calm."

No thinking mind can read this marvelous incident and fail to see both sides of the Son of God, both the human and the divine. It seems to me that He had been up all the night before running the great healing meeting at Capernaum, and, now He starts across the Sea of Galilee and He is almost exhausted, and the human side needs rest, and while the little ship is being tossed on the bosom of Galilee, Jesus falls asleep, and while He sleeps, a mighty storm arises and the waves begin to roll over the ship, and the disciples become frightened, run to their sleeping Lord, and awake Him, saying, "Lord, carest thou not that we perish?" and He arose and rebuked the wind and the sea, and every blue-breaker on Galilee went back into its hole like scared rats, and the Christ stood there in mid-ocean on the deck of that little ship master of every situation.

We see again that nobody but a man could go to sleep on a floating ship, but nobody but God could arise and rebuke the storm and wind and have them to obey Him. How beautifully this incident brings out His personality and divinity! The twenty-seventh verse says that the men marvelled. I don't wonder, do you? How could they help but marvel to see the blue breakers rising over their boat one minute and the next minute see the Sea of Galilee looking like a sea of glass, and not a breaker in sight. The men said, "What manner of man is this, that even the winds and the sea obey him!" Of course they marveled, and they haven't stopped yet.

Reader, that was the same Jesus that spoke peace to my troubled soul. Bless His dear name! He has been breaking up storms for these many years, and when I see what I am now and what I used to be, and then see what I am going to be, of course I marvel just like the rest of the men.

Now, we have just been looking at Jesus on the boat in time of the storm and saw what He did, now let us watch that little boat land, and see what He does. Let us begin in the 28th verse and read a few verses. "And when he was come to the other side into the country of the Gergesenes, there met him two possessed with devils, coming out of the tombs, exceeding fierce, so that no man might pass by that way. And, behold, they cried out, saying, What have we to do with thee, Jesus, thou Son of God? art thou come hither to torment us before the time? And there was a good way off from them an herd of many swine feeding. So the devils besought him, saying, If thou cast us out, suffer us to go away into the herd of swine. And he said unto them, Go. And when they were come out, they went into the herd of swine: and, behold, the whole herd of swine ran violently down a steep place into the sea, and perished in the waters." Of course they went. No devil ever hangs around when Jesus tells him to go.

Now some truths connected with the lesson. First, these devils were so fierce that no man could go by where they lived; second, there was a man that paid them a visit and he proved to be an old acquaintance of these devils; third, they got their plunder ready and made arrangements to move before the boat landed; fourth, they knew Jesus was coming before He left Capernaum; fifth, the devil got up the storm on Galilee to defeat the purpose of the Son of God, but when Jesus commanded the wind and the sea to be still, and they obeyed Him, the devil knew that he was the fellow that was defeated; sixth, the very fact that the devils cried out and said, "Art thou come hither to torment us before the time?" proves that they knew Him, and I feel in my heart that just a few minutes before the boat landed the devils told the men in whom they resided that they had just as well commit suicide, for they never aimed to leave them in this world, and at the same time these devils had their duds all ready and had one eye on the boat, and the other on the hogs, but they were in hopes that these men would destroy themselves until they saw the Son of God step from the deck of the little ship, and then they cried out and said, "Art thou come hither to torment us before the time?"

The very fact that they referred to the time proves that the devil knows that he only has a limited time to work, and that the day has already gone down on God's calendar when Jesus is to destroy his works; so, knowing these facts, they begged Jesus to let them go into the herd of swine, and now yonder goes the devil with a hog skin on, and there sit two men at the feet of Jesus clothed in their right mind, telling Him of the awful experience they had had with the devils in them, driving them from home and friends and bringing them into the tombs, and how glad they must have been to find themselves once more free from the devil and looking the Son of God in the face, and rejoicing in a Saviour's love.

These men knew that they had met God, and peace and joy flooded their souls, and now the sad thought of their beautiful story. After Jesus had done so much for these men that were a trouble to the whole country, the people rose up and wanted the meeting to stop at once, and besought the Son of God to depart out of their coast, and the Book tells us that He went, and we have no account of His ever coming back. How strange it is to think that they would want Him to leave the coast for several years! No doubt these two men devil-possessed had been so bad no man could go by where they stood, and now the people see them with shining faces sitting at the feet of Jesus, in their right mind. It seems to us the whole neighborhood would have rejoiced together, but how different! The people rose up in a solid mass and demanded that the revival stop and that Jesus Christ get out of the country as soon as possible. I say with a sad heart that I have seen some revivals where Jesus Christ was without a doubt casting out devils and the people rose up and demanded the revival to close, and besought the evangelist to depart out of their country, so there is not much difference between some of the people of Texas, and the Gergesenes.

We read now in the opening of the ninth chapter, "And he entered into a ship, and passed over, and came into his own city. And, behold, they brought to him a man sick of the palsy, lying on a bed: and Jesus seeing their faith said unto the sick of the palsy; Son, be of good cheer; thy sins be forgiven thee. And, behold, certain of the scribes said within themselves, This man blasphemeth. And Jesus knowing their thoughts said, Wherefore think ye evil in your hearts? For whether is easier, to say, Thy sins be forgiven thee; or to say, Arise, and walk? But that ye may know that the Son of man hath power on earth to forgive sins, (then saith he to the sick of the palsy,) Arise take up thy bed, and go into thine house." And he arose, and departed to his house. But when the multitudes saw it, they marvelled, and glorified God, which had given such power unto men" Matt. 9:1-8.

Some beautiful things in connection with this lesson: He left the Gergesenes and came to His own city, and they brought Him a man sick of the palsy. He first saw the faith of the men that brought the sick man, next He forgave his sins; third, the scribes reasoned in their hearts; fourth, He read their thoughts; fifth, He healed the palsy in their presence, and sent the man home with his bed on his shoulder to convince the people that He could forgive sins! sixth, the multitude glorified God; seventh, I see the old scribes sneaking off, while all the saints shouted for joy.

We next notice from the eighteenth to the twenty-sixth verses of the ninth chapter, "While he spake these things unto them, behold, there came a certain ruler, and worshiped him, saying, My daughter is even now dead: but come and lay thy hand upon her, and she shall live. And Jesus arose, and followed him, and so did his disciples, And, behold, a woman, which was diseased with an issue of blood twelve years, came behind him, and touched the hem of his garment: for she said within herself, If I may but touch his garment, I shall be whole. But Jesus turned him about, and when he saw her, he said, Daughter, be of good comfort; thy faith hath made thee whole. And the woman was made whole from that hour. And when Jesus came into the ruler's house, and saw the minstrels and the people making a noise, he said unto them, Give place: for the maid is not dead, but sleepeth. And they laughed him to scorn. But when the people were put forth, He went in, and took her by the hand, and the maid arose. And the fame thereof went abroad into all the land."

We see here the Son of God starting to raise to life a dead girl, and before He got to the home of the ruler to raise his daughter to life, we find a woman who had been afflicted for twelve years, come in behind Him, and touch His garment. She was made whole of her plague. A double miracle. It seems that He started to the home of the ruler, but between the points from where He started and the home of the ruler, there was evidently a woman waiting for Him. The Book does not say that He knew she was there, but I am sure He did, and I believe He went right by where she was on purpose to give her a chance.

I believe that when any man or woman gets on the road side to wait for the Son of God, He always goes by. And she did not have to wait long, for Jesus knew she was a needy case, and by the time she got seated on the roadside, Jesus came up and was walking by her as though He saw her not, but she saw Him and came in behind Him and touched His garment, and was made whole, and Jesus turned Him about and when He saw her He said, "Daughter, be of good comfort, thy faith hath made thee whole," and the woman had the greatest day of her life. I am satisfied in my mind that she went on with Him and the disciples to the home of the ruler to see Him raise the dead girl, and while He was putting out the sinners and unbelievers, getting ready to raise the girl, this woman shouted all the time, and after the girl was raised to life, I think they all stayed till after dinner, and this woman that had been an invalid for twelve years was one of the waiters at dinner. I think she waited on the Lord and shouted with the girl.

We next notice from the twenty-seventh to the thirtieth verses: "And when Jesus departed thence, two blind men followed him, crying, and saying, Thou son of David, have mercy on us. And when he was come into the house, the blind men came to him: and Jesus saith unto them, Believe ye that I am able to do this? They said unto him, Yea, Lord. Then touched he their eyes, saying, According to your faith be it unto you. And their eyes were opened." You notice it says that when Jesus had departed these two blind men followed Him. No doubt they were in the community and heard of the great meeting in the home of the ruler, and started to the meeting but before they reached there, the meeting had closed and Jesus had left. They followed on after Him crying and saying, "Jesus, thou Son of David, have mercy on us." It seems that He went into the house to wait for them to come on and overtake Him, and when they came in, He said unto them, "Believe ye that I am able?" And they said, "Yes, Lord." And He said unto them, "According to your faith be it unto you." And thank God their eyes were opened.

We next notice the thirty-second and thirty-third verses: "As they went out, behold, they brought to him a dumb man possessed with a devil. And when the devil was cast out, the dumb spake: and the multitudes marveled, saying, It was never so seen in Israel."

Here is another beautiful miracle, the casting out of the devil and enabling the dumb man to speak. What a Christ we have! Healing the woman, raising the dead maid, opening the eyes of two blind men, casting out a devil, and restoring speech to a dumb man, all in a single day!

Now we read in the thirty-fifth verse, "And Jesus went about all the cities and villages, teaching in their synagogues, and preaching the gospel of the kingdom, and healing every sickness and every disease among the people." I suppose He must have healed thousands of folks, too many to call special attention to them all. A few cases were described to let us see what He could do and what He did do, and to show us what He wants to do.

The last verses of the ninth chapter close with the fact that "when he saw the multitudes, he was moved with compassion on them, because they fainted, and were scattered abroad, as sheep having no shepherd." And He asked the disciples to pray that the Lord might send other laborers into the vineyard, for said He, "The fields are white unto harvest, but the labourers are few." And the same loving, tender Voice is calling out to us today—to not only do all we can for a lost and perishing world, but to pray that the Lord of the harvest may send other laborers into the harvest fields to gather in the golden grain for the garners above, and then He said, "We shall come rejoicing, bringing in the sheaves," and I say, Amen.

In the tenth chapter of Matthew, we have the calling of the twelve apostles and their commission to go into the cities of Judea. They were forbidden to go among the Gentiles, or the Samaritans, but were commanded to go to the lost sheep of the house of Israel. Now, we have noticed that up to this point, Christ had done all the work Himself; all the miracles have been performed by Christ, but now He says to His apostles, "And as ye go, preach, saying, The kingdom of heaven is at hand. Heal the sick, cleanse the lepers, raise the dead, cast out devils: freely ye have received, freely give."

We see in this commission that Christ is including a part of His burden, or taking His work and transferring it to men, for up until now, He had done all the work and had His disciples to stand by and look on while He did the work, but now He gives the first commission to mortal man to go and do the work of a God.

The reader will see that to heal the sick, cleanse the lepers, raise the dead and cast out devils is a work beyond the human unaided by the divine, for we know that humanity without divinity can never restore a dead man to life. It takes supernatural power to do these things, but I want the reader to notice that these disciples were to only go to the Israelites, or the lost sheep of the house of Israel, and into any of the cities of the Gentiles or Samaritans enter ye not; but you will remember that when He started back to the right hand of the Father He told these same men to "wait for the promise of the Father, which, saith He, Ye have heard of me," and then He said, "Ye shall receive power, after that the Holy Ghost is come upon you: and ye shall be witnesses unto me both in Jerusalem, and in all Judaea, and in Samaria, and unto the uttermost part of the earth."

Now, reader, you will notice that the first commission these disciples received was only to the Jews, but after they were baptized with the Holy Ghost and sanctified they were to go to the whole world, and bring them a glad message of a full gospel that was world-wide, beginning at Jerusalem. There are many beautiful things in the eleventh, twelfth and thirteenth chapters that I would love to notice, but this sermon would grow too long.

There are a few wonderful miracles recorded in the fourteenth chapter that we want to call your attention to. We see the Son of God standing on the mountain side, sunburnt and dust-covered, preaching His own everlasting gospel, while the mountain seems to be literally covered with the hungry multitudes, hanging on His words, so carried away with the message, that they just simply refuse to go away to get food until the disciples become alarmed, and fear that the whole multitude will perish with hunger, and they go to Jesus and ask Him to send the multitude away, that they may go into the towns and cities and buy themselves victuals, but Jesus said to the disciples, "Give ye them to eat, ye need not send them away." And one of the disciples said, "Lord, two hundred pennyworth of bread is not sufficient for them, that every one of them may take a little." And Jesus said, "How many loaves have ye here?" and they say, "Five barley loaves, and two small fishes," and He said, "Make the people sit down," and He said, "Bring the loaves and fishes to me," and He offered thanks and blessed the bread and fish and brake and gave to His disciples, and they to the multitude, and they did all eat and were filled, and there were five thousand men besides women and children. They gathered up twelve baskets full of the fragments that were left over.

The reader will notice that none but a man could stand on the mountainside covered with dust and preach the gospel, but while that is true, none but a God could bless five loaves and two fishes and feed twelve or fifteen thousand hungry people. How beautifully the wonderful miracles bring out the humanity and divinity of Jesus Christ.

We next notice that as soon as the multitude was fed that Christ told the disciples to go down and get into a ship and cross over Galilee to the other side, and that He would send the multitude away; and we read that the disciples went down and got into the ship, and started across to Bethsaida and that He sent the multitude away, and went alone into the mountain to pray. While the disciples were crossing Galilee, a great storm came up and we read that He saw them struggling and rowing against the wind, which was contrary.

Now, we next read that He went out to them walking on the sea about the third watch of the night. I suppose it was about three o'clock in the morning, and while the blue breakers were rolling up against the little ship, Jesus came walking by them. We read that He made as though He would go by, and when they saw Him, they cried out, and He said, "Be not afraid, it is I," and when Peter heard that it was Jesus, he said, "Lord, if it be thou, bid me come unto thee on the water," and Jesus said, "Come," and Peter walked on the water to go to Jesus, but we read that when he saw the waves, he began to sink, and cried out, "Lord, save, I perish," and Jesus pulled him up out of the water and said, "Wherefore didst thou doubt, O thou of little faith?" Jesus came up into the ship and the storm ceased, and immediately the boat was at the land.

Well, Amen. We see that when the Lord's children are in a storm, He is always watching them; second, He always comes by; third, He comes in, if He is wanted; fourth, the storm always ceases when He comes in; fifth, the little boat was landed immediately after Jesus came in.

We only have space for one other miracle of our Lord. We turn now to the eleventh chapter of St. John's gospel and read that when Lazarus had been dead four days already Jesus stood at his grave with the broken-hearted sisters, and Martha said, "Lord, if thou hadst been here my brother had not died." And Jesus said, "Thy brother shall rise again," and Martha said, "I know he shall rise in the resurrection at the last day." Jesus said, "If thou wouldst believe, thou shouldest see the glory of God." And he wept with her and Mary, and then said, "Take ye away the stone." And Martha's heart failed her and she said, "Lord, by this time he stinketh," and Jesus said unto her, "Said not I unto thee, if thou wouldest believe, thou shouldest see the glory of God?" And then took they away the stone. And Jesus lifted up His eyes unto heaven and said, "Father, I thank thee that thou always hearest me," and then He said, "Lazarus, come forth." And he that was dead came forth, bound hand and foot. Jesus said unto them, "Loose him, and let him go."

This miracle of Jesus Christ is the capstone of all His wonderful works. How wonderful it seems to think of a man who had been dead four days, getting up and walking out of his grave, bound hand and foot, and how it shows Jesus Christ to be both human and divine! See Him standing by the grave with Mary and Martha, weeping like His heart would break, but hear Him, as He says, "Lazarus, come forth," and see a dead man come to life. He weeps like a man, but He raises dead men like God.

Strange Critters

When we look around us we find three places of abode; this world, heaven and hell. Man first appears in this world, and stays but a short time, just long enough to prepare for one of the other two places of abode, and in a short time, he will emigrate to one of these places to spend eternity.

These two places that we call heaven and hell are both very peculiar places. They are both prepared places and no man can enter either of these places without a preparation for that special place. When a man comes into this country and begins a preparation for heaven, if he lives to be three score and ten, it takes him all his life to prepare for that special place. If he undertakes to prepare for hell, it will also take him a lifetime to prepare.

The preparation for heaven is holiness of heart and life. The preparation for hell is a life of sin and unrighteousness. No man can get into heaven with any sin in him; and no man can get into hell with any holiness in him. God will not allow sin to enter heaven, and the devil will not allow holiness to enter hell. The thing God loves is holiness, and the thing He hates is sin; and the thing the devil loves is sin, and the thing he hates is holiness. I am like the Lord to the extent that I love holiness and hate sin, and I am not like the devil to the extent that I hate holiness and love sin.

God is never satisfied with a man as long as there is one thing in his heart that is unholy, and the devil is never satisfied with a man as long as he has one desire in his heart to be pure and holy. With these facts before us, it makes us tremble to go into some churches and see how bad people hate holiness, while they claim to be the children of God. If I hate the thing God loves, and love the thing God hates, it seems to me that it would be awfully uncomfortable for me to be thrown into the presence of God to stay for a few million years, and with that verse in the

Bible where it says, "How can two walk together except they be agreed?" Why, it looks to me like the fellow would become so dissatisfied in heaven right in the presence of God where he could hear nothing but, "Holy, Holy, Holy, Lord God Almighty," that he would just simply get up and leave the city.

If a man hates holiness, it would be just as distasteful to him in heaven as it would be in Texas, and to go from Texas to heaven would no more change the man's moral nature than to go from Texas to Arkansas. The human family found out long ago that changing localities did not change the moral side of man in the least, and the human family found out also that it is not the place a man is in that makes him happy, or unhappy, but the condition he is in morally.

If sin is an unrestful element, in the heart of man in this country, wouldn't it be, if possible, a thousand times more so in heaven? Think of a man going to heaven with sin in his heart! Don't you know it would make him so miserable that he would try to commit suicide by jumping into the River of Life.

If a little holiness meeting here in this world puts people under conviction and they become so wretched and miserable that they go to fighting holiness to try to relieve their guilty conscience, what on earth would a fellow like that do, if he was turned loose in heaven? All classes of religious people talk of going to heaven, and you can tell them of their dead kinfolks over there, and they all want to go right away, and you tell them to come to the altar and let God make them holy, and it is to a great many an insult to speak to them on the subject of scriptural holiness.

My friend, that proves to my mind that if the great bulk of church members were to go to heaven and meet their kinfolks in the holiness move over there, they would be as badly dissatisfied there as they are here. The heaven they have wanted to come to for so many years has at last been reached, and to their surprise they find that the very thing that gave them so much trouble here in this country is all over heaven, and that heaven is just a place of holiness, where every saint and angel shouts, "Holy, Holy Holy, Lord God Almighty! The whole earth is full of Thy glory."

O my friend! if Bible holiness is distasteful to you, go down before Him that sitteth on the throne, and let Him cleanse away everything in your heart that opposes holiness, for if there is an unrestful, unsatisfied thing in your heart, you must get rid of it in this country, for the very fact that there is something in your heart that hates holiness, proves that this very something would hate God, and tear Him from the throne, if it was possible.

We can see further with our eyes shut than we can with them open. Our enemies despise us, and yet honor us. The deeper down we go, the higher up we get; the more we give away, the more we have left. Our sun shines as bright at twelve o'clock at night as at twelve o'clock in the day. Alive to the world and dead to God; alive to God and dead to the world. We were set free in order that we might become servants. When we broke the law, we were bound by the law. When we kept the law, we were free from the law. His strength is made perfect in our weakness. We glorify Jesus by helping the other fellow. We have more for ourselves when we divide with our neighbor.

WE ARE STRANGE "CRITTERS."

"By honour and dishonour, by evil report and good report, as deceivers and yet true; as unknown and yet well-known; as dying and behold, we live; as chastened and not killed; as sorrowful, yet always rejoicing; as poor, yet making many rich; as having nothing, and yet possessing all things." We overcome by yielding; we talk the loudest when we say nothing; we keep all we give; and we lose all we keep; we have found out that the way up is down; we find that the nearest cut to the heart of our neighbor is to go clear up by heaven. We win the battle when we surrender; we walk on earth and live in heaven; we are in the world, and yet not of the world. When we are weak then are we strong; we conquer the enemy when we refuse to fight; we run faster on our knees than we do on our feet.

The Unselfish Christ

He gave everything and kept nothing. He gave heaven for a stable; He gave His throne in the skies for a bed in an ox trough; He gave up His reputation when He left heaven and came to dwell among men; He put on humanity to enable us to put on divinity; He became the Son of man that we might become the sons and daughters of the Almighty; He became the Light of Life; He became meat that He might feed the perishing; He became the Bread of Life that a hungry world might eat and live forever; He became the Water of Life that the thirsty might come to Him and slake their thirst and go on their way rejoicing; He became rest for the weary, and said, "Come unto me, all ye that labour and are heavy laden, and I will give you rest"; He became riches for the poor, for we read "by his poverty, we shall be made rich"; He became sleep for the sleepy, for we read, "And so shall he give his beloved sleep"; He gave His peace to His disciples, He said, "My peace I give unto you, not as the world giveth, give I unto you; let not your heart be troubled, neither let it be afraid"; He gave His joy to His disciples, He says, "Ask that your joy may be full." Jesus Christ is the only chief man the world ever heard of that had a surplus of joy and peace left over to be used and enjoyed by His followers. Other men have left money and houses and land, but the Son of God left His joy and peace to His friends. He gave sight to the blind; He gave healing to the afflicted; He gave life to the dead; He made the world, and then came into the world and was not known in the world and had no place to stay while He was in the world, and He came to His own and His own knew Him not. He gave His clothes to His enemies; He gave His back to the smiters and His cheek to them that pluck off the hair, and hid not His face from shame and spitting. His visage was so marred, more than any man's, and His form, more than the sons of men. He gave His life for the world, and tasted death for every man. He gave Himself for the church that He might sanctify it, and cleanse it with the washing of water by the word that He might present it to Himself a glorious church without any spot or wrinkle, or any such thing, but that it should be holy and without blemish." He shall never fail. He shall not be discouraged. He shall see of the travail of His soul and shall be satisfied. He was patient with His enemies; when they struck Him in the face, He gave them a look of kindness and only said, "Why smitest thou me?" He was patient with His friends; when they wanted Him to set up an earthly kingdom He only said, "My kingdom is not of this world."

While He was dying, His enemies mocked Him and said, "If thou be the Christ, come down from the cross, and we will believe on you." He only said, "Father, forgive them, for they know not what they do." The only things the world ever gave Jesus were a crown of thorns, a Roman scourge, and gall mingled with vinegar. That shows their love for Him.

Evangelists and Holiness Workers

Some of the evangelists and holiness workers as I have seen them. First, a flock of white doves: M. L. Haney, L. B. Kent, Isaiah Reid, E. Davies, Dr. Foote, Dr. P. F. Bresee, and Dr. Daniel Steel. As I have looked into the faces of these old heroes, they looked like they were half glorified, while they were yet living; their hair is almost as white as snow, and their character is whiter than their hair. They have been filled with the Holy Ghost until they don't look like they belonged to this world. They really look like they belonged to some other planet, and I am sure they do; and I expect to meet them on that planet.

We next notice the big four. The four greatest preachers that I have ever met and heard preach the gospel are H. C. Morrison, B. Carradine, C. J. Fowler, and Joseph H. Smith. These four men are without doubt the greatest preachers that walk on the earth. I just simply yoke them up together and call them the "big four." They stand head and shoulders above the general rank and file of our good preachers. We have many very excellent preachers in the holiness ranks, but they are not quite up with the big four, and the reader will remember that I am just describing these men as they appear to me.

The big seven is a Bible number, and bless the Lord, they come in as follows: Seth C. Rees, E. F. Walker, B. W. Huckabee, G. W. Wilson, A. M. Hills, L. L. Pickett and A. A. Niles. These men rank at the very top of the ladder in preaching ability, and for sweetness of life and character, they are not surpassed in the United States of America. They are great soul-winners and are doing a great work in the Holiness ranks, and have been a blessing to many thousands of Adam's fallen race, and, no doubt, will be the means of bringing tens of thousands more to the foot of the cross. Even so, Amen. I am believing for it and expecting it to come to pass.

We notice next the big six: D. F. Brooks, John Hatfield, W. W. Hopper, L. L. Gladney, C. W. Ruth, E. A. Fergerson. These men are great teachers and fine preachers and very successful soul-winners. They just simply have a revival all the year round. They never go out of business or hang their harps on the willows, but they beat their drums and sing and shout and lick the enemy anywhere in this country. They are a holy terror to the devil and his kingdom.

The eleven young giants of the holiness movement, Will J. Huff, H. W. Bromley, W. J. Harney, John Paul, Andrew Johnson, I. G. Martin, John L. Brasher, C. E. Cornell, Chas. M. Dunaway, James W. Pierce, and C. K. Spell. Now, these young men are the coming young men in the holiness ranks. There are just hundreds of fine young preachers in the holiness movement, but I refer to these, as a few out of the great rank and file, who are just simply great preachers. These young men can preach anywhere on the American continent, and carry their end of the stick and never have to look down their noses.

Now, I want to go over some of these men and yoke up some of them in a different light, and see how beautifully they work together. Now, let me show you four cyclones of fire: H. C. Morrison, Seth C. Rees, E. A. Fergerson and John Hatfield. These four men are the flames of fire in the holiness ranks. They burn into white heat and burn a hole into everything that gets into their way. In fact, a man on fire for God has but a few things in his way. A man on fire generally has his own way, for people don't bother with fire much. If you sit down on a chunk of fire it will burn a blister on you.

The four cyclones of honey are B. Carradine, honey in the rock, Joseph H. Smith, honey in the comb, C. W. Ruth, and D. F. Brooks. These four men stand at the head when it comes to sweetness of life and experience. While they have all the fire and unction they need, yet the leading characteristic of their lives is their loving, gentle, sweet, winning way. Their sermons are made up of sunshine, laughter and tears. They are a wonder to the world in which they live. I don't think I ever saw one of them without a smile on his face or a tear in his eye. They are God-called, God-sent and Spirit-filled men.

The four great teachers are W. B. Godbey, A. M. Hills, L. L. Pickett and E. F. Walker. Now these four men will stand on any platform on earth and teach with any set of men on earth. I mean just what I say. These men are qualified to teach anywhere, and to meet any set of men on any religious doctrine that is taught on earth. They are all great preachers and soul-winners, and among the finest revivalists in the holiness work. They are broad-minded, level-headed men, filled with the Spirit, and true and tried, and doing a great work for the cause they love so well.

The three greatest reasoners in the holiness work are Dr. C. J. Fowler, A. A. Niles, and George W. Wilson. These men are at the head of their class on this line. I have heard these men reason until my head almost popped, and when they closed the gate they had every sheep in the pasture and every goat on the outside. Dr. Fowler has been properly called "logic on fire." I suppose when it comes to a logical conclusion, he is the Pike's Peak of America. He just simply puts his big bald head over everything that walks on dirt and breathes wind. I give him the white belt.

The four men in the holiness work that had no sugar or candy or honey put into their make-up at all are B. S. Taylor, John H. Appell, R. M. Guy, and W. G. Airhart. These men are all backbone, but their breeches are made out of galvanized iron, but no four men in the holiness ranks stand higher or live straighter than these men, and while they are all backbone, the bone seems to be made out of kindness, and when you need a favor, these old boys are ready with hand and pocketbook both. They are among the elect of the earth, and I expect to shine and shout with them forever.

Some of the most untiring workers in the holiness work of Texas are R. L. Averill, J. T. Upchurch, C. B. Jernigan, E. C. DeJernett, C. M. Keith and C. A. McConnell. These old boys have stood against the odds and stood in the hard places and have never surrendered one point to the devil. While we have a great many fine workers and preachers in Texas, these six soldiers for years have been at the front of the battle. I am sure Bro. R. L. Averill has done more hard work in Texas than any man in the holiness movement for fifteen or eighteen years. That old boy has very seldom ever been out of a holiness revival. He has championed the holiness cause in Texas as no other man.

Now a word about our holiness singers. The greatest singers in the holiness work are J. M. and M. J. Harris, Charlie D. Tillman, Charlie Weigele, W. B. Yates, L. L. Pickett, Mrs. Flora Phillips, Arthur Johnson, Rose Potter Crist, John M. Waters, C. B. Jernigan, and Asbury Dean and wife. Now, of course, there are a great many more splendid singers that I have not worked with, but these singers can all be found and counted on as fine leaders of song service. They are Spirit-filled singers, and their work is in constant demand from one end of America to the other the year around.

Well, before I close my sketch about the evangelists there is one man I want to speak of, and that is Bro. Joseph H. Smith. I have already referred to him but not as fully as it should be. Now, without a doubt, Joseph H. Smith is the greatest Bible teacher in the holiness movement, and I am persuaded that he has not a superior in the United States, and as far as I know, there is no man on earth that is his equal. He is the giant of America. When it comes to explaining the Scriptures, he just simply stands at the head of the column. He is like Saul, the son of Kish. He is head and shoulders above all in his tribe.

It Makes No Difference What a Man Believeth, Just so He Is Honest in It

You will find my text this morning in the book of Deception, in the seventeenth chapter and forty-fourth verse, and it reads as follows: "It makes no difference what a man believeth, just so he is honest in it." This is no doubt one of the biggest guns that the devil ever shot. A non-believing world and a half-believing church with the very face of the text shows it to be one of the biggest lies that was ever hatched out of the old nest eggs from under the mud sill of perdition, and it was set on and hatched out, and feathered out, and shipped out by the devil himself, and it is unloaded at every station in life from the cradle to the grave, and you will find it on every street corner, and in almost every business block in every city in this great nation of ours. Now, we read about the dispensation of the Father and the dispensation of the Son, and also a great deal about the dispensation of the blessed Holy Ghost, all of which are lovely and beautiful to the man or woman who has been born again and sanctified wholly, and filled with all the fullness of God, but without a doubt in my mind, and we are living now in a moonshine dispensation. I mean by a moonshine dispensation that the great bulk of the religious teaching of our day will not measure up to God's standard and requirements at His judgment bar; and that when the needle eye of Gabriel pierces the consciences and the unregenerated hearts of men, who emphatically deny every statement of God's Word, and teach a salvation without regeneration, and a Christianity without Christ, and when they stand at the flaming bar of God, they will drift away like the pale shimmering moonshine before the rising sun on a June morning.

It was God who raised a high standard; it was men who tore it down. It was man who raised a low standard; it is God who will burn it down. God says, "Ye must be born again." Man says, "We don't believe in such nonsense as a new birth; it is perfectly absurd and disgusting to our refined sensibilities to talk of being born again." God says, "Be ye holy, for I am holy." But man says, "I don't believe in holiness. I saw a man that said he was holy and he was a crank. Why, he got up in church and walked the floor and clapped his hands and shouted. You could have heard him several blocks, and it was disgusting to us and we put him out and forbade him to ever come to our church again." God says, "Without holiness no man shall see the Lord." But man says, "Holiness is contrary to human nature, and I never saw one, and nobody has ever been able to show me one." And man says, "I don't believe in holiness and I am honest in what I believe."

Oh, yes, we hear that everywhere we go, that it makes no difference what a man believes, just so he is honest in it. We have a great multitude who tell us that they don't believe in the Bible and that they are honest in it, and they tell us that they are perfectly sincere in what they believe. But right in the face of what they don't believe, they tell us that they are perfectly honest in it.

The old Book says, "He that believeth on the Son hath everlasting life, but he that believeth not, the wrath of God abideth on him." But the fellow rises up and says, "If I can't believe God and I am honest in it, would God be so cruel as to put me in hell?" Well, the facts are that God will never put you there, you put yourself there. "He that believeth hath eternal life." And you say you don't believe, therefore, you shut the gate of heaven in your own face. Faith in the Lord Jesus Christ opens the gate of heaven, and unbelief shuts it, and you are a free agent to think and act for yourself, and if God says, "Ye must be born again," and you say you don't believe it, and God says, "Ye must be holy," and you say you don't believe in holiness, if you were to go to heaven in that condition and were to have to spend an eternity in the presence of the God you had failed to believe, heaven would be an awful hell to you. Just imagine a man who had broken every command given, and disbelieved every word of the Bible, and laughed at the new birth and made fun of holiness, and is taken right up into the presence of the God he had rejected. Don't you know heaven would be worse than hell to such a man, and hell or no hell, fire or no fire, brimstone or no brimstone, there is no place in the universe of God but that man would rather be in, than in the presence of God.

Well, now we take another step in the text. Remember it reads, "No matter what a man believes, just so he is honest in it." We have a great multitude who tell us that they only believe the Bible in part, and they look right into the face of God and dispute His Word and tell Him to His face, that there are whole books and half books, and whole chapters and half chapters, and many verses and words, that they don't like, and they reserve the right to go through God's Book and tear out all that don't just suit them, and by the time they all get through tearing out what don't suit them, we have no Bible left. They all tell us that they are perfectly honest in what they believe and right in the face of all their honesty, as they tear up the Bible, God says that if any man takes one thing from His book that his part shall be taken out of the Book of Life, and that if he adds anything to the Book that all the plagues that are written in this Book shall be added to the man's life. The land is flooded with these critics, and they have entered the church of Jesus Christ, and stand in the pulpits of the land and even claim to be preachers of the gospel. I wonder whose gospel? Not the gospel of Jesus Christ, for His "gospel is the power of God unto salvation to every one that believeth," and they are unbelievers. Therefore, they are not preachers of the gospel of Jesus Christ, but the cry comes back from every quarter of the globe, "We don't believe all the Bible. We only believe the part that suits us, and of course we are honest in what we believe. Therefore, we have a perfect right to undermine the faith of God's children, and take their Bible away from them, and leave them nothing but our opinions, because we are honest in what we believe, and we don't believe in the new birth, and we don't believe in the baptism with the Holy Ghost, and we can't stand Christian perfection at all, but we are perfectly honest in what we believe. Therefore, both the world and the church should take off their hats to us, because we are honest in what we believe, and we believe that the three great dispensations of the Father, Son and

Holy Ghost are all three fulfilled and passed away, and that we are now in the glorious dispensation of the moonshine age, and we are honest in what we believe."

We next notice that God said that He created the heavens and the earth and all things that exist; that He also created man in His own image, and after His likeness; but we see a great company that tell us that away back somewhere a little speck came into existence and floated on, and finally was changed into a small insect, and floated on and was changed into a small creeping thing, and floated on until it was changed into a walking thing; and it walked on and became a monkey, and the next change was the baboon age; the next thing was the ape age; from them man in all his glory sprang into existence, and he is now the monarch of the universe. They show us that man sprang from nothing, and that he is going to nothing, but somehow, it is hard for us to believe that, when the old Book tells us that God created man for His own glory, and that we can know God while we live and glorify Him in our souls and bodies, which are His, and then live with Him forever in the blessed land of light.

Now these fellows tell us that they don't believe that God created the universe, and created man, and started him out a holy being. They tell us that they are honest in what they believe, and they tell us that they are evolutionists, and just can't believe in the creation as we find it in God's Book, but the text says it makes no difference what a man believes, just so he is honest in it. But thanks be unto God, the old Book says that God created the heavens and the earth, and that He created man in His own image, and I am ready to confess that the Bible account of the creation is the most reasonable one I ever heard. But these boys rise up and say, "Now what are you going to do with me? I am perfectly honest in what I believe." Well, now, we will look at your case, old boy, and tell you just what we think. The Bible says that God created man in His own image, and put him in the garden of Eden with his beautiful wife and told them, "Multiply, and replenish the earth," and of course, if you sprang from the monkey that proves that you did not spring from man. Therefore, you are a well developed monkey. You are not a man at all, and have no part nor lot in the interests of the children of God, and when you die you will go to the place where all dead monkeys go. I am not sure just where that place is. You monkeys will have to settle that between yourselves. We, the sons and daughters of the Almighty, are going to heaven, the country prepared for all God's people, who believe the Bible and believe God.

We next notice a great crowd of people that tell us that they don't believe in the divinity of Jesus Christ. They say He was a good man, but not divine. They laugh at the atonement and make fun of the blood, and say that they are saved by His life, and they mock Him in His dying struggle on Calvary, as He redeemed a lost world from death and hell. They tell us that they received all things from God, the Father, and only use the life of Christ as a model to go by. They say preaching the blood of Jesus Christ is so disgusting and distasteful to them that it is an insult to their refinement and their cultured sensibilities, and for decency's sake, they can't listen to a discourse on the blood of Christ, but the old Book says "without the shedding of blood there is no remission of sins."

Now listen! We are redeemed by His blood; we have our sins forgiven through His blood; we are justified through His blood; we are washed through His blood; we enter His church through His blood; we are cleansed by His blood; we enter into the holiest by His blood; we are sanctified by His blood; we are made perfect in love by His blood; we are elected by His blood; we overcome the devil through His blood; we join the blood-washed army through His blood, and now, reader, all this great mob of blood-rejecters and Christ-despisers are howling up and down this land, telling us that they are honest in what they believe, when I have heard them with my own ears and have seen them with my own eyes mock and hiss at me as I preached on the atoning blood of a crucified Son of God, for the sins of a lost world, and they had enough sin and hell in their faces to damn a universe, while they mocked at the shed blood of the Son of God, at the same time claiming to be honest in what they believe. They call themselves Unitarians, or Christ-rejecters, but honest in what they believe.

The next crowd described in the text tells us that man is so good and great and lofty that he cannot be lost. It makes no difference what God and the Bible say, that man is just simply too good to be damned. They ignore God and idolize man, and dispute every word in the Bible, and break every commandment that God ever gave to the world, and in the face of God and His revealed word, go on preaching a universal salvation. They tell you that all men will be saved, but God says, "He that believeth shall be saved, and he that believeth not shall be damned."

Why, reader, the man that disputes God's word will break God's law and reject God's promises. If he were to get to heaven, he would have trouble there in the first twenty-four hours after he arrived, and yet they tell us that they are honest in what they believe.

The next crowd we notice in the text tells us that they have found out that God and the Bible are both mistaken. That there is no devil, no sin, no hell, and no matter only mind, no laws, no pain, only a delusion in the mind. If your ankle bone was broken and not set right, and grew back crooked, that the ankle was all right—it was only an optical delusion, and that man when he was boiled down proved to be more than an ox liver, hanging up in the butcher shop, just a big piece of jelly with a long swallow on one side and a gall on the other. They have rejected God and His word and yet claim to get good light from the God they have rejected. They have rejected the Bible and written one of their own, which denies that awful thing of sin.

God said in His Book that every imagination of the human heart was only evil continually, but the above crowd tells us that there is no such thing as evil, and they go on down the stream of time with a mighty host of followers, plunging into outer darkness without God. For God says, "How can two walk together except they be agreed?" And God says, "Repent ye and turn from your evil ways, for why will ye die?" And they shout back in God's face, "We have no evil to repent of"; therefore they are not with God in this world, and will not be in the one to come, but still they tell us that they are honest in what they believe; but what kind of honesty is it? In the name of Jesus Christ, brother, see what you believe?

Papers and Schools

The Pitcher of Cream is not complete without a sketch of our papers and schools which go in to make a part of the cream of the holiness movement.

We will first notice the Texas Holiness University. This remarkable school was founded in 1899. A number of good men and women were interested in it: Bro. E. C. DeJernett, B. A. Cordell and W. G. Airhart, with a good many others, but I suppose Bro. DeJernett did more to get this school on foot than any other man. I think the devil has charged it up to DeJernett. And while Bro. DeJernett prayed and worked, other good men came to the help of the Lord. The Lord put it into the heart of Bro. B. A. Cordell to give the land, and he gave forty acres for the school; and from that hour the school has been on a boom for God and lost souls. In May of 1899, the brethren met in the name of E. C. DeJernett and elected a board of trustees and called a president, Dr. A. M. Hills of Oberlin, Ohio, being called to this position, and coming right on to Texas before the week closed. He was on the ground and met with the brethren and planned the work, and for six years he was president, until in the summer of 1906 he resigned to become president of the new school at Oskaloosa, Iowa.

From the time Dr. Hills resigned, the school has been without a regular president, although Prof. L. B. Williams has been acting as president.

This school has had a most remarkable history in its seven years. More than fifteen hundred people have either been converted or sanctified, and the school has grown from an opening with twenty-seven students, to nearly four hundred, and from twenty-five different states. Much more could be said that would be of interest to the public, but space forbids our saying more.

We next notice Asbury College, located at Wilmore, Ky. This school was founded by J. W. Hughes, a Southern Methodist preacher, some twelve or fourteen years ago, and as far as we know, Asbury College was the first real holiness school in the United States. Old Asbury College is the mother of all the other holiness schools in America. When Brother Hughes established Asbury, he had no idea what a blessing he was bringing to the world and the people of America. Many men and women have gone out from Asbury to bless, not only the people of America, but in all parts of the world, they have gone to tell the story of full salvation, and eternity alone can tell the good of the work done by Brother Hughes when he founded Asbury College.

*　　*　　*　　*

We next notice the two schools at Meridian, Miss., owned and run by J. W. Beeson, and Dr. M. A. Beeson. First, Bro. J. W. Beeson started this school for young women. I have been all over the country, and I want to say it is my opinion that Bro. J. W. Beeson has one of the best and safest schools for young women on the American continent. Now he don't know that I am writing this sketch, but out of a heart full of love for all the schools I am writing.

I think he started a few years ago with a handful of girls, perhaps twelve or fifteen boarding students. Now he has over five hundred girls with their heads and bodies and souls all looked after in a most beautiful way. Beeson is turning out well-rounded women. No school is doing more to develop womanhood than the Female College at Meridian, Miss.

Some three or four years ago, Bro. J. W. Beeson and his brother went in together and bought the old Baptist college, which is now doing a fine work, and is building up in a wonderful way. The Doctor has had some bad luck, as the world would call it. All his buildings burned down, but in the end it will prove to be a blessing to him, for all of the old buildings were wooden structures, and when they burned, Bro. Beeson rose up and built good brick buildings, which will, in the long run prove to be a blessing instead of a curse. He has two hundred and fifty young men, and is doing fine work. This is the only holiness Male College in the holiness movement, I think, and his brother has the only Female College. In a few years, these two schools will run up to a thousand students; seven or eight hundred are enrolled in both schools.

* * * *

We next notice Taylor University at Upland, Ind., with Dr. C. W. Winchester at the head. Taylor is doing fine work, and is turning out young men, who will be a blessing to our nation. I think they have from two hundred and fifty to three hundred students enrolled, and the school is a great spiritual power, that is felt all over Indiana and adjoining states. And with such men as Dr. Winchester at the head of affairs, there is a bright future ahead for the Taylor University.

* * * *

We next notice the Holiness College at Ruskin Cave, Tenn., with Professor Smith at the head. This is a new school, only two or three years old, but Brother Smith is a fine scholar and a great teacher, and he is building up a fine school, and in a short time he will be turning out young men and women prepared to fill any avocation in life. The school is very spiritual and is one of the pitchers of cream in the holiness movement, and in a few years, Bro. Smith will have the school second to none in the South, for he is a very fine educator, and his school will come to the top in the near future.

* * * *

We next notice the Central Holiness University, located at Oskaloosa, Iowa, with Dr. A. M. Hills at the head. This school bids fair to become one of the strongest and the best holiness schools in America. In the first place, twenty-five years ago, the

Lord sanctified Isaiah Reid, and for twenty-five years Bro. Reid has been laying plans for a great work among the holiness people, and Iowa is one of the best organized states in the holiness work. And when the time came for Iowa to establish a holiness school, the people were ready for the emergency, and with their prayers, faith and money, they rose up to build, and the first year, they planned to put up seventy-five thousand dollars' worth of buildings, and opened the school in September, 1906, with one hundred and fifty students enrolled the first month; and with Dr. A. M. Hills at the head, they are going to build up a great school, for Dr. Hills is one of the strongest men in the holiness move, and he is one of the finest teachers I know of connected with the holiness work. Therefore they are going to have a great school. While Isaiah Reid may not be known as connected with the school, yet he has been going up and down in Iowa organizing the holiness people into state and county associations for twenty-five years, which means so much now to a move on foot when united action is wanted, for if the people will pull together, we know they will succeed, and in so doing, we can see what a blessing it has been to the people of Iowa for some man to spend years in organizing them and getting them ready when the time came to rise and build. Well, amen, thank the Lord for what is being done in the great holiness move for the cause of Christian education; and without a doubt the holiness schools are the best examples of Christian education in the world.

*   *   *   *

We next notice Kingswood College located at Harned, Ky. Bro. J. W. Hughes, the founder of Asbury College, is also the founder of Kingswood. Bro. Hughes sold out Asbury to a board of trustees, and he is now at the head of a new school, which bids fair to become a great and useful school. Bro. Hughes is a strong teacher and full of energy, fire and life, and with twelve or fifteen years of experience in the college work, he will soon have a great school at Kingswood. It will be remarkable to see what he will do in the next two or three years. I understand he has a fine location and wide field to build up in. Well, the Lord bless Brother Hughes, and give him a prosperous time, and build up his school until he will have another Asbury on hand, as I believe he will.

* * * *

We next notice the holiness school located at Vilonia, Ark., with Prof. C. L. Hawkins at the head. Bro. Hawkins is a graduate of Asbury College and taught two years, I think, in the Texas Holiness University. He is in a fine field for a good school. Arkansas is ripe for holiness, and I understand that Brother Hawkins has built up a fine school there, and is doing a good work, and has a revival almost all the time in his school. Well, amen. See what God has wrought in a few years.

* * * *

We will now proceed to speak of the holiness papers. We will begin at home again, for the Old Book says to begin at Jerusalem. A few years ago, the Lord put it into the hearts of a few of the boys to establish the *Texas Holiness Advocate*; I think, seven or eight years ago. The *Advocate* has grown until it has about four thousand subscribers, and has been honored of God, and has been a great factor in the building of the holiness move in Texas, and also of the Texas Holiness University. Bro. C. M. Keith was its editor for five or six years. For more than a year, Rev. B. W. Huckabee has been the editor in chief, with Brother Charlie McConnell as office editor. The *Advocate* is progressing, the people of Texas love the *Advocate*, and it has done more to build up the holiness people in Texas than any other one thing. May it live long and bless the world as it grows and spreads.

* * * *

We will now look at the *Pentecostal Herald*; and when we see what the *Herald* has done for the great holiness movement of the South and Southwest, we are constrained to glorify God. I am convinced that no paper or man in all the Southland has done as much for the great holiness movement as Brother H. C. Morrison and the *Pentecostal Herald*. Brother Morrison has been editor of the *Herald* ever since it was founded. He started there a number of years ago without money or subscribers, and he worked, prayed, saved and economized, and put his money, brains and heart into the *Herald* until he has by far the greatest religious paper in the south, and H. C. Morrison and the *Pentecostal Herald* have fought more great battles for the holiness cause than all the other papers in the south. And, again, he has done more to beat back worldliness and ungodliness in the church than any ten preachers or papers who were not friendly to the holiness cause. The Lord only knows where the M. E. Church, South, would have drifted to when they went to opposing holiness, if some man had not stood in the gap, and for nearly twenty years, Bro. Morrison has stood between the old church, and the awful breakers. Although he has been peeled and blistered, he has stood firm for the doctrine of the church, and now the *Herald* has a great circulation, and is read by many thousands of people each week, and no paper ever published has stood firmer for the doctrine taught by old John Wesley, and the early Methodists, than the *Pentecostal Herald*. May the *Herald* live and grow until it will find a lodging in every home in this great Southland, is the prayer of one who loves the *Herald*.

* * * *

We next notice the *Christian Witness*, published by Drs. C. J. Fowler and G. A. McLaughlin. The *Witness* is to the north and northwest what the *Pentecostal Herald* is to the south and southwest. The *Witness* is a strong paper, has a large circulation, and is as straight on the doctrine of holiness as a gun barrel. For many years the *Witness* has stood for full salvation when she had to stand alone; and when the preachers of the north closed up on the doctrine of the church and started in the wrong direction, the *Witness* was on the ground to champion the cause of righteousness and ring the dinner bell to a full gospel, and there is no telling what a strong paper, north or south, has been worth to the hungry multitudes. In fact, what would become of the poor hungry sheep if they did not get a holiness paper once a week? O how I do praise the Lord for the fact that God in His divine providence has provided for the people to have a full gospel, if not from the pulpit, thank the Lord, from the press.

* * * *

We next notice *The King's Herald*, published in Louisville, Ky., Rev. L. L. Pickett, editor. *The King's Herald* has a good large circulation and is one of the most readable papers published. We have no writer that is more instructive than Bro. Pickett. No paper has more good things in it than *The King's Herald*. It is loaded down to the water-line with the choicest holiness news every issue, and it fairly sparkles with sunshine and grace on every page. May it live long to bless the world.

* * * *

We next notice *God's Revivalist*, published by Mrs. M. W. Knapp, of Cincinnati, O. This paper was started by Brother M. W. Knapp, and published by him until he was taken to heaven. Brother Knapp was one of the leading men in the great holiness work, and as a preacher and writer, there was none better than he. Since God, in His divine providence, took him to his reward, his wife has been carrying on the good work he so nobly started and carried on while he lived. The *Revivalist* is one of the strongest holiness papers published, and has one of the largest circulations of any holiness paper in the field. It is a strong, clear paper on the doctrine of Scriptural holiness, and is a great blessing to the people of America, and is also a mighty factor in the great missionary work in several foreign nations. May God's richest blessings rest upon Sister Knapp and her paper till Jesus comes and she goes up.

We next notice the *Way of Faith*, published at Columbia, S. C., by Bro. John M. Pike. The *Way of Faith* is an excellent paper with a fine circulation, and is doing a great work down in the southland. Bro. Pike is a strong preacher and a fine writer, and he is a fine editor, and is doing a great work for God and the great cause of holiness he loves so well. May Brother Pike and the *Way of Faith* live to bless the world until Jesus comes, and then, by *the way of faith*, may he go up with a shout in his soul, is my prayer.

* * * *

We next look at *Living Water*. This paper is published by J. O. McClurkan at Nashville, Tenn. Brother McClurkan is getting out a fine paper, and is doing an excellent work. He is running *Living Water* on the line of foreign missions, and is building up a strong paper, with a large circulation. The *Living Water* is a fine paper and is strong and clear on the subject of holiness and is much loved and appreciated by the holiness people in the South. Brother McClurkan is a fine preacher and a strong writer, and has a fine field to operate in, and the Lord is using him in fine work among the holiness people.

* * * *

We next notice the *Christian Standard*, published by E. I. D. Pepper and Son. The *Standard* is published at Philadelphia, Pa., and also at Gainesville, Fla. This paper is one of the strongest papers, and is read by thousands of people in America each week. The reader will remember that Dr. Pepper has been at the head of the Mountain Lake Park Camp Meeting for many years, and by his work through the *Standard* and Mountain Lake Park, Dr. Pepper has been a blessing, not only to the people of America, but to the world at large. May the blessings of God be upon the *Standard* and its editor until we meet him in the clouds and rejoice together to see our Lord Jesus Christ.

We next notice the *Nazarene Messenger*, published at Los Angeles, Cal., by Dr. P. F. Bresee. The reader will remember that Dr. Bresee is the founder of the Church of the Nazarene, and the *Nazarene Messenger* is the organ of their church and is a fine paper, well gotten up. It is building up a fine circulation, and no man has dared as much for the cause of Scriptural holiness on the great western shores as Dr. Bresee. For many years he has stood like the Rocky Mountains in that far off western country. May he and his paper live long to bless the world is the prayer of one who loves him.

* * * *

Now for the lack of time and space, we will have to lump a few papers together. Brother Nelson at Indianapolis and Brother Sherman at St. Louis, and the Holiness Christ Church, are all getting out fine papers. These publications are good and doing a great work, and God smiles upon them, and they are doing a fine work in the great cause for holiness and are a blessing to the people. Brother Sherman's paper is the *Vanguard*. The Holiness Christian Church is publishing *The News of Glory*. Brother Nelson is publishing *The Pentecost Herald*.

* * * *

Now reader, I have just briefly referred to the leading holiness schools and papers. I was not able to go into all of the leading details of either the schools or papers, and there are several other smaller papers and schools which I haven't time or space to mention, but they are doing a fine work, and they all go in to make a part of the cream of our great holiness move which is the greatest religious move on earth.

* * * *

And now may our schools and papers grow until they will fill the world with the knowledge and glory of God as the waters cover the sea. I wish I could be connected with every school and paper; not that I am worthy, but love them so well and want to see them succeed.